Unlocking Small Business Ideas

An idea is the first step in the process of creating a business. Most ideas, no matter how brilliant they may seem, never actually end up becoming a business. This book explains how to:

- Look for new small business ideas.
- Evaluate ideas for their commercial potential.
- Unlock the strategies that turn an idea into a business.

English's focus is on finding the seed of an idea and the process of developing it into a genuine business opportunity. He includes practical diagnostic 'reality checks' developed in his small business workshops. He also includes an analysis of changes in the Australian small business environment as a result of Covid-19.

This practical volume is ideal for any budding entrepreneur looking for guidance on how to evaluate a business opportunity and build a commercial strategy around it. It will also be an ideal secondary reading for books on entrepreneurship and small business courses.

John W. English brings together a lifetime of business insight as an academic, entrepreneur, and author. As Associate Professor in Entrepreneurship and Deputy Director in the Australian Innovation Research Centre at the University of Tasmania, he introduced undergraduate and postgraduate programmes in entrepreneurship and commercialisation. As a consultant to government agencies in Australia, New Zealand, and the United States, he conducted start-up workshops on how to assess new ideas for their commercial potential. He is the author of the bestselling book *How to Organise and Operate a Small Business in Australia*, now in its 11th edition.

Unlocking Small Business Ideas

An Australian Guide

John W. English

Routledge
Taylor & Francis Group

LONDON AND NEW YORK

Designed cover image: © Getty Images

First published 2023
by Routledge
4 Park Square, Milton Park, Abingdon, Oxon OX14 4RN

and by Routledge
605 Third Avenue, New York, NY 10158

Routledge is an imprint of the Taylor & Francis Group, an informa business

© 2023 John W. English

British Library Cataloguing-in-Publication Data
A catalogue record for this book is available from the British Library

ISBN: 9781032496443 (hbk)
ISBN: 9781032496436 (pbk)
ISBN: 9781003394808 (ebk)

DOI: 10.4324/9781003394808

Typeset in Bembo
by Apex CoVantage, LLC

Disclaimer

The information contained in this book is, to the best of the author's knowledge, true and correct. Every effort has been made to ensure its accuracy. The author does not accept any liability for any loss, injury, or damage caused to any person acting as a result of the information in this book or for any errors or omissions.

Contents

Introduction

We are in the midst of a new era in which the jobs of the 21st century are being created by people who run their own businesses. Small businesses can be found in all industries, but the most spectacular growth is taking place in personal and professional services, online businesses, and skilled trades. Incomes range from a few dollars each week to over a million dollars a year. Their goal is not just to make a living but also to create a sustainable business that provides a comfortable lifestyle for themselves and their family. At last count, there were over two million actively trading small businesses in Australia. Each one began with an idea!

Those who are inspired to have their own business are usually looking for a lifestyle that will give them interesting, stimulating, and challenging work. They want control over their time, including the flexibility to take time off when they wish. Many people prefer to work part-time without the responsibility and stress of a full-time job. A small business is one way of achieving these goals while at the same time providing the income to support an enjoyable standard of living. The reasons that lead people to start their own businesses are just as diverse as the businesses themselves.

- **Lifestyle choice.** Are you looking for a way to gain greater control over your work–life balance? Do you want to be autonomous, operate by your own rules, and have the freedom to decide when and where you will work?
- **Career change.** Do you have a distaste for wage slavery in a large company or public sector organisation? Do you yearn for something smaller, simpler, and more personally gratifying?
- **Home business.** Home businesses are popular among individuals who want to earn a living while staying close to home. The reasons might range from needing to care for other family members to the convenience of not having to commute for work.
- **Retirement business.** The Baby Boomer generation is entering retirement, and increasingly, they have been starting businesses. According to the Reserve Bank of Australia, the proportion of business owners over the age of 55 has nearly doubled in the past five years. A small business offers

DOI: 10.4324/9781003394808-1

the prospect of an exciting change of pace as well as a tremendous way to stay engaged and remain productive. Many of these businesses operate on a part-time basis.

- **Intentional entrepreneur.** Are you the dreamer and the free spirit who has always wanted to have your own business? When you find the right business opportunity, you can test it by starting out on a small scale.
- **Accidental entrepreneur.** Have you been cast adrift in mid-career as a result of corporate or public sector restructuring? Are you looking for a way to use your talents, skills, and experience to set up your own business?
- **Limited job prospects.** Have you found yourself in a dead-end job with little chance of improvement? Some individuals consider starting a business out of necessity because their employment prospects are limited.

More than half of the small businesses in Australia are one-person operations called *solo businesses*. They typically take advantage of outsourcing some functions while focusing on their core strengths. They have no responsibilities for employees, they are in complete control of the business, and the profits belong solely to themselves. Relatively inexpensive and powerful computers, voice mail systems, mobile phones, the Internet, and e-mail have made the solo business functionally feasible and financially realistic.

A small business is a very special way to earn a living. Countless Australians have gone down this path, and for many, it has been a source of happiness and prosperity. Whatever the underlying reason, the key ingredient is a genuine desire to create a business. Those who take the plunge expect to benefit from the advantages of having their own business.

- You can be your own boss, you can be independent, and you can exercise your own talents and capabilities.
- You can develop your own ideas and work on something that is personally satisfying.
- You will have the chance to make money, maybe even a great deal of money, and you will not be dependent on a fixed wage or salary.
- You will have the prospect of achieving a feeling of personal worth, accomplishment, and recognition.

An idea is the first step in creating a business. It can emerge unexpectedly, or you might stumble upon it inadvertently. What happened to your last idea? Do you remember it? What did you do with it? Ideas typically come and go without much thought. But what if they didn't? ***Unlocking Small Business Ideas*** is intended to be your navigational guide to identifying an idea and turning it into a flourishing business. It describes how to look for small business ideas, how to evaluate an idea for its commercial potential, and how to transform an idea into a genuine business opportunity. The book is divided into four parts.

Part A is about unlocking an idea. It explains a practical approach to spotting new ideas, assessing their commercial potential, and creating a blueprint for turning them into a business. It also describes what you need to do to get started and where to look for help. Part A concludes with a reality check to help you identify and evaluate an idea's potential risks.

Part B is about unlocking a marketing strategy. It includes how to create a marketing strategy, how to use conventional marketing methods, and how to take advantage of digital marketing methods. Part B concludes with a reality check to help you evaluate the prospects for capturing a target market.

Part C is about unlocking an operating strategy. It explores key issues in organising service operations, online operations, retail operations, and manufacturing operations. Part C concludes with a reality check to help you identify and evaluate potential operating constraints.

Part D is about unlocking a financial strategy. It includes how to control cash flow, how accounting systems work, and how to interpret financial information. It also describes how to obtain finance and how to comply with the Australian taxation system. Part D concludes with a reality check to help you decide if the financial projections make sense.

The book concludes with an appendix that combines each of the reality checks into a Commercial Feasibility Rating. It provides feedback about your idea to help you make an informed judgement about whether there is enough commercial potential to pursue it further. It is an exercise that can be repeated whenever you make changes that are intended to improve the commercial potential of the idea.

Part A

Unlocking an idea

Unlocking an idea begins with a search for ideas, testing the ones you find to see if they have commercial potential, and mapping out a blueprint for commercialising the one you choose. The blueprint lays out all the important start-up requirements for getting into business and there are many sources of advice and assistance available to help you along the way. All ideas carry some degree of risk, so it is important to make an early assessment to determine if you think they are tolerable.

Chapter 1 focuses on the process of turning ideas into business opportunities. It considers how the pandemic has affected the business landscape, how to go about spotting new ideas, how to assess the commercial potential of ideas, and how to create a blueprint for commercialising an idea. The chapter concludes with an example of a blueprint for a one-person, home-based, online business.

Chapter 2 explains the essential start-up requirements. These include selecting a legal structure, applying for an Australian Business Number, registering a trading name, applying for a Tax File Number, getting all the necessary licenses and permits, finding premises if you need them, making sure you are properly insured against business risks, and what to expect if you decide to employ staff.

Chapter 3 shows you where to look for help and assistance. It includes professional advisers like your solicitor and accountant, local support such as a business mentor or a Business Enterprise Centre, a trade association for your type of business, state and territory government support, and Commonwealth government support.

At the end of Part A, there is a reality check in which a series of questions is used to identify and evaluate the potential risks of commercialising an idea. External risks include compliance risk, technology risk, economic risk, political risk, and dependence risk. Internal risks include planning risk, marketing risk, deliverables risk, liquidity risk, and personal risk.

DOI: 10.4324/9781003394808-2

1 Turning ideas into opportunities

The pandemic had a big impact on how businesses operate, leading to fresh concerns about health and safety, a rapid uptake of digitalisation, and a renewed emphasis on buying locally. With this in mind, we are looking for product ideas, service ideas, market ideas, and occasionally a genuinely radical idea. Not all ideas are good ideas, however, so a method for assessing ideas for their commercial potential is presented. Creating a practical blueprint for commercialising an idea significantly improves the prospects for a successful business. It is the key to making a smooth transition from the initial idea to a going concern. It identifies the target market and the plans for making sales, the day-to-day procedures for running the business, the financial results that can be expected, and a checklist of things that are needed to become operational.

Pandemic legacy

The pandemic crisis has culled a lot of outdated business practices. It has fundamentally changed how and what people buy, and it has accelerated many of the structural changes that were already underway. Customers still want to shop, travel, eat out, be entertained, and socialise. How they engage in these activities, however, has been affected by the pandemic experience. Three key trends resulting from the pandemic are health and safety, going digital, and buying locally.

Health and safety

The pandemic has focused everyone's attention on health and safety. Some people remain hesitant to venture out of the house or take part in activities where they previously felt exposed. Others are making fewer visits inside businesses because of their concern about coming in contact with others and jeopardising their health. Customers have these concerns in the back of their minds, and health and safety should be part of every post-pandemic business strategy.

Most businesses have already implemented procedures to protect the health and safety of their customers. Whether it is a restaurant, a retail outlet, or holiday accommodation, the key is to demonstrate that health and safety are a priority.

DOI: 10.4324/9781003394808-3

Things like more frequent and effective sanitising, limited in-store interactions, convenient contactless ways to order and pay for goods, and options for pickup or delivery are important to post-pandemic customers.

Going digital

The digital revolution was already well underway when the pandemic accelerated major changes in how customers engage with businesses. A lot of people tried online grocery shopping for the first time, and many have permanently converted to this way of shopping. Customers now know what is possible online, they have the tools to take advantage of what it offers, and they are increasingly comfortable using them. These are major and lasting changes in which new habits have been formed and new expectations have been created. It sends a strong signal that an online presence is now an essential element in practically every business strategy.

More than half of small businesses in Australia don't have a website, despite the fact that most of the population is connected to the Internet. These businesses are missing out on a massive amount of exposure, and they are losing sales. Before the digital revolution, the options were essentially limited to print and media advertising. Today, the Internet has changed everything. There are social media platforms, websites of all kinds, downloadable apps, email, and more. Even businesses that don't sell directly online can use the Internet to get customers' attention.

Technology has provided an essential lifeline to individuals and businesses during the pandemic, and perceptions of its value have increased. People are creatures of habit, and these new behaviours have become habits. The issue is not more technology; it is what you can do with it. If you are serious about being in business in the post-pandemic era, then you need to approach every aspect of your business with a digital mindset. Visit *business.gov.au/asbas* for information about how you can access individual support through ASBAS Digital Solutions. This government programme offers small businesses low-cost, high-quality advice on a range of digital solutions to meet their business needs.

Buying locally

When the pandemic disrupted supply chains, people began looking for local suppliers to fulfil their needs. They are now accustomed to the convenience of nearby businesses and local markets. For these loyal customers, it is not price or product variety that is most important, it is the novel ways in which they have adapted to the post pandemic environment. For example, businesses that offer delivery options such as curb side pickup or free contactless delivery have enjoyed enthusiastic support. Many local businesses moved to online sales during the pandemic in an effort to recuperate losses and stay in business. Whether it was on their own platform or through social media, the increases in online sales have demonstrated that customers have embraced local businesses that joined the digital revolution.

Spotting ideas

It isn't necessary to discover a unique idea or come up with an invention involving some enormous leap of the imagination. There is simply no correlation between commercial success and the creative or technological brilliance on which an idea is based. Ideas can consist of modifications to products or services, finding new markets for existing products or services, or inventing something new.

Product ideas

Product ideas consist of improving, developing, or acquiring a product aimed at a particular target market. For example, organic and environmentally friendly versions of well-known consumer products are product ideas. Introducing a domestic version of an industrial product is a product idea. Product ideas that are totally new are exceedingly rare. Typically, it is much easier to look for an existing product that has the potential for one or more of the following modifications:

- enhancing its quality
- broadening or narrowing the range offered
- improving usability, performance, or safety
- changing the delivery method, packaging, or unit size
- adding new features, accessories, or extensions
- simplifying or making it more convenient
- increasing access, portability, or disposability
- changing colour, material, or shape
- making it larger/smaller, lighter/heavier, or faster/slower.

Service ideas

A service business performs a task for the customer. The task generally requires specialised training, experience, or equipment. The key drivers of service ideas are productivity and reliability underpinned by expert knowledge, skills, and experience. Some ideas are focused on the person providing the service, while others are focused on specialised equipment to deliver the service. Service ideas tend to follow one of three strategies. Standardisation is a service strategy that minimises costs, maximises productivity, and produces a uniform service. Flexibility is a service strategy aimed at providing a broad range of customised services. Penetration is a service strategy designed to offer several services to the same customers. Look for ideas that are valued, affordable, and capable of being effectively advertised and promoted.

Market ideas

Market ideas consist of finding new customers for existing products or services. It may be a different geographical area, a different type of customer, or a different distribution method. Franchising has been a spectacular example of new market ideas with thousands of franchisees operating across a variety of markets. When you see a successful business concept in another place, consider the possibility of applying the same idea in your market. Also, keep in mind that a website can give you access to markets all over the world.

Radical ideas

A radical idea is a completely new product or service. It is radical because the idea is novel, and it has the potential to upset the way in which established products or services have previously operated. These are typically new inventions that take a long time to develop and are costly to bring to market. The risks are extremely high, but if you get it right, so are the rewards. Radical ideas are a combination of foresight and chance. Some radical ideas are *pushed* by technological developments, but the majority are *pulled* into existence by a market that is looking for them.

Assessing commercial potential

A genuine business opportunity is an idea with compelling commercial potential. Some ideas have commercial potential, but many don't. The question is how to tell them apart. Assessing commercial potential consists of a practical evaluation of the potential risks involved, the capacity to capture a market, possible operating constraints, and the expected financial outcomes.

Potential risks

External risks have the potential to restrict the commercial potential of an idea. Can it comply with the various legal, safety, and other regulatory requirements? Is it vulnerable to changes in technology? Is it exposed to changes in the economy? Will it be affected by government policy? To what extent could sales depend on factors that are beyond your control? Internal risks are different because you can take steps to manage them. Have you got a plan for making the transition from the initial idea to a business operation? Are you sure you thoroughly understand what customers want? Is it possible to produce and deliver the product or service in the way it is intended? Will there be enough money to make it through the start-up phase? Can you withstand the pressure on your personal finances, your career, your family, and your emotions? Questions for identifying external and internal risks are presented at the end of Part A. Together, they provide a reality check on the risk profile of an idea.

Capturing the market

Anticipated demand is one of the most important elements in evaluating an idea, and it is also one of the most difficult to assess because it requires an understanding of customer behaviour. It's not about forecasting sales at this early stage; it's about painting a picture of the factors that push demand. What do you know about the relative size of the target market? Is it increasing or decreasing? Will demand be stable or unstable? How long will demand for this idea last? What scope is there to extend this idea into other products or services?

Market acceptance is important in converting anticipated demand into sales. It affects the rate of adoption and the extent to which the market can be captured. There are a variety of reasons why customers may accept or reject an idea. Does it fulfil a genuine need? Can prospective customers easily recognise the benefits? Is it compatible with their existing attitudes or patterns of use? Is it complicated to consume or use? Will it be difficult or costly to distribute?

Market strength is concerned with how an idea is likely to fare in the battle of the marketplace. How is the idea different from similar products or services? How will customers value it compared with similar products or services? Is it vulnerable to the negotiating leverage of customers? Is it vulnerable to the negotiating leverage of suppliers? Is it susceptible to existing, potential, direct, or indirect competitors?

Questions for evaluating anticipated demand, market acceptance, and market strength are presented at the end of Part B. Together, they provide a reality check on an idea's capacity to capture its target market.

Operating constraints

Successfully commercialising an idea depends on having the right expertise and resources to exploit it. This includes marketing, technical, financial, operational, and managerial expertise. The relative importance of each depends on the sophistication of the idea and the nature of the market it faces. Exploiting an idea also depends on having access to the right resources. Resources complete the basic dimensions of an operations strategy, including financial resources, physical resources, human resources, critical information, and access to help and assistance. Questions for evaluating the expertise and resources required to commercialise an idea are presented at the end of Part C. Together, they provide a reality check on the constraints on operations and where additional expertise and/or resources are needed.

Financial projections

Having identified the best mix of expertise and resources puts you in a position to see if an idea makes financial sense. The starting point is a realistic forecast of sales revenue. Given the level of activity in the sales forecast, a projected balance sheet reflects what assets are needed to operate the business and how they can be financed. A projected income statement reveals if the idea is profitable and how long it might take to break even. Finally, a cash flow budget tells you if there is going to be enough money to sustain the business until it becomes cash flow positive. A reality check for evaluating the financial projections are presented at the end of Part D.

Creating a blueprint

A blueprint sets out how you will make the transition from an idea to a going concern. It's not rocket science. It is the result of a little research and a big dose of common sense. It identifies the characteristics of the ideal customer and how you intend to capture them. It includes your methods for generating sales, the day-to-day procedures for operating the business, and the financial results you expect to achieve. The questions that follow are designed to help you structure your blueprint.

- What is my business? What type of business do I intend to enter? What will I call it, how will it be organised (as a proprietorship, partnership, or company), and what will be its main activities?
- What is my product or service? Exactly what am I going to sell? Is my product or service already on the market, or is it still in the development stage? If it is in the development stage, what is the roll-out plan to bring it to market? What factors make this product or service unique or superior? Will there be opportunities to develop related products or services? What will it cost to make/buy/provide the product or service? Can I price the product or service competitively and still earn a good profit?
- What is my target market? There are four steps in determining the nature and size of the target market.

  - Who are my customers? Are they individuals, households, or businesses? Why will they buy my product or service?
  - How big is the target market? How large is the pool of prospective customers? What are they likely to spend on my product or service?
  - Who are my nearest competitors? What do I know about their operations? What will be my competitive strength? What share of the market do I think I can capture?
  - Based on the previous steps, what sales do I think I can realistically expect?

- How will I generate sales? How will I stake a claim to the target market? How will I satisfy my customers' needs? What will be my pricing policy, and what will be my methods for promotion and distribution?

- How will I operate? What is the plan for getting organised and into operation? What equipment, stock, or other resources will I need to acquire? What materials or supplies do I need? What are the day-to-day processes and procedures that I will set up? Who will do the work? If I have staff, will they need to be experienced, or will I provide training? What functions can I outsource? How can I use technology in my operation?
- What are my financial projections? Financial projections are primarily concerned with cash flow. The objective is to be confident about the financial viability of the business. Make sure the projections are not overly optimistic. Initial financial projections typically consist of your expected sales, your start-up and operating expenses, and the amount of cash you will need to sustain the business until it becomes cash flow positive.

What follows is an example of a blueprint for a one-person, home-based, online business. It is simple, brief, and informal.

Toddler togs online

My name is Catherine Grace, and I live in an Australian capital city. I worked for a clothing manufacturer as a pattern maker for five years after I left school. When my children were toddlers, I used my skills to design and make all of their clothes. I now have over 400 unique patterns for children aged 1 to 4 that I would like to sell online. I intend to operate the business part-time from my home.

MARKETING STRATEGY

I will offer sewing patterns for toddler clothing from my own website. The patterns will be delivered online as a PDF file, and they will include a list of fabrics and notions together with step-by-step sewing instructions. Each pattern includes sizes 1 through 4, and it can be printed on a home printer using A4 paper. The price per pattern is $9.90 including GST.

The patterns are copyrighted and will be sold as a licence to download, save, and reprint them for personal use. Personal use includes small-scale production in a home business for sale in a local market. The licence does not include forwarding, copying, or otherwise distributing the PDF file, or using it in production outside the home on a commercial scale. The target market for *Toddler Togs Online* sewing patterns consists of three main segments.

- Mothers with toddlers who want to sew clothing for their own children using these unique designs.
- Individuals who enjoy sewing and want to use these designs to make clothing for the children of relatives and friends.

- Individuals who want to use these designs as part of a home-based business to make garments can sell them in local markets or on online platforms such as Etsy.

When *Toddler Togs Online* becomes established, there are opportunities for expansion. One possibility is to sell complete kits that include the pattern and instructions, fabric chosen from a list, and any required notions. The Internet makes it possible to reach markets globally, and another possibility is to target customers outside of Australia.

The mainstay of my marketing profile will be my website. It will feature a complete portfolio of my patterns, including high-resolution photos and detailed descriptions. It will be searchable across a variety of themes. It will also contain answers to frequently asked questions and articles related to sewing for toddlers together with a blog in which customers can share their experiences. The website will be fully functional to handle online purchases. My objective is to steer online visitors to my website without using paid advertising. I intend to do this in several ways.

- While the majority of sales are expected to come from my website, I will also offer patterns on Etsy, a virtual marketplace for handmade articles. I will do this to make Etsy visitors aware of my website.
- The social media sites that are popular with my market segments will be investigated, including Facebook, Pinterest, Twitter, and Instagram, in addition to specialist social media platforms aimed at people who are interested in sewing.
- The first pattern will be offered free to visitors who register on my website and agree to join my email list. This will not only create their account but also enable them to see and evaluate a pattern with no risk.
- I will produce a quarterly newsletter distributed by email. It will feature one of the themes in my collection together with any new designs. It will also have a link back to my website for more information.

OPERATING STRATEGY

Each pattern will be digitised by scanning the hand drawn pieces. The .jpg files will be edited in Photoshop and combined into a complete pattern in the form of a PDF file. Each of the four sizes will be in a different colour, making it easy for the user to cut out the size they want.

I intend to hire a professional website designer for the development of my website. I have a quotation from Wombat Web Weavers for the design and installation of my website for $10,000. It includes registering my domain name and building a website that includes a shopping cart, checkout, and online payment facilities. It also includes installing my website on a hosting service and training me to maintain it.

The website will contain pictures and descriptions of more than 400 patterns. Customers will be able to view the patterns and choose the ones they want by placing them in a shopping cart. When they are ready to complete their purchase, they will proceed to the checkout to enter their account details and email address. They will be able to make payments through PayPal, Visa, or MasterCard. When payment has been accepted, a link to the pattern will be sent to their email address. Using the link, they will be able to download the pattern and instructions using Adobe Reader, save them to their computer, and print them out on any home printer that uses A4 paper. If any pattern piece is larger than A4 paper, it will print out as two sheets that can be joined together.

FINANCIAL PROJECTIONS

I have $20,000 in savings that I am prepared to invest in the business. Before I can begin operations, I will need to pay $16,250 in start-up costs. The cash flow forecast for the first year begins with modest sales that gradually increase to 500 downloads per month. Most of the expenses (except 'Other fees') remain the same regardless of the level of downloads. I don't intend to take any money out of the business during the first year.

The Year 1 cash flow forecast shows negative cash flow for the first three months, becoming cash positive in the fourth month. At the end of twelve months, the net cash position is forecast to be $20,541. If the actual result is similar to the forecast, I shall withdraw $20,000 out of the business and return it to my savings.

The Year 2 cash flow forecast assumes that sales will remain constant at 500 downloads per month. I have done this to demonstrate that the business is sustainable with no further growth while generating $3,000 per month in drawings. The Year 2 forecast will be recast at the end of Year 1 to reflect what I have learned during the first twelve months and any plans I may make for further expansion.

CHECKLIST OF THINGS TO DO

- Register a business name.
- Register an ABN.
- Register for GST.
- Install an NBN service and a business landline.
- Find an available domain name and reserve it.
- Set up an email account.
- Open a business bank account and a merchant account.
- Open a PayPal account.
- Ask my accountant to set up a simple accounting system.
- Check to see if I need any business insurance.
- Ask my solicitor to draft the terms and conditions for downloads.
- Ask Wombat Web Weavers for a draft contract for the design and installation of my website. Ask my solicitor to review it.
- Set up my social media accounts and link them to my new website.
- Research my competitors including their offerings, prices, and websites.

TODDLER TOGS ONLINE

FORECAST CASH FLOW YEAR 1

	Before start-up	July	Aug	Sept	Oct	Nov	Dec	Jan	Feb	Mar	Apr	May	June	Total
Receipts														
Downloads		25	50	100	150	200	250	300	350	400	450	500	500	3,275
Dollar sales		248	495	990	1,485	1,980	2,475	2,970	3,465	3,960	4,455	4,950	4,950	32,423
Starting cash	20,000													20,000
Total	20,000	248	495	990	1,485	1,980	2,475	2,970	3,465	3,960	4,455	4,950	4,950	52,423
Disbursements														
Hardware	5,000													5,000
Website	10,000	250	250	250	250	250	250	250	250	250	250	250	250	13,000
NBN	500	350	350	350	350	350	350	350	350	350	350	350	350	4,700
Other fees	750	19	37	74	111	149	186	223	260	297	334	371	371	3,182
Sundries		100	100	100	100	100	100	100	100	100	100	100	100	1,200
BAS				1200			1200			1200			1200	4,800
Drawings														
Total	16,250	719	737	1,974	811	849	2,086	923	960	2,197	1,034	1,071	2,271	31,882
Net cash flow	3,750	−471	−242	−984	674	1,132	389	2,047	2,505	1,763	3,421	3,879	2,679	20,541
Cash position	3,750	3,279	3,037	2,053	2,726	3,858	4,247	6,294	8,799	10,562	13,983	17,862	20,541	20,541

TODDLER TOGS
ONLINE

FORECAST CASH FLOW YEAR 2

	July	Aug	Sept	Oct	Nov	Dec	Jan	Feb	Mar	Apr	May	June	Total
Receipts													
Downloads	500	500	500	500	500	500	500	500	500	500	500	500	6,000
Dollar sales	4,950	4,950	4,950	4,950	4,950	4,950	4,950	4,950	4,950	4,950	4,950	4,950	59,400
Total	4,950	4,950	4,950	4,950	4,950	4,950	4,950	4,950	4,950	4,950	4,950	4,950	59,400
Disbursements													
Hardware													
Website	250	250	250	250	250	250	250	250	250	250	250	250	3,000
NBN	350	350	350	350	350	350	350	350	350	350	350	350	4,200
Other fees	375	375	375	375	375	375	375	375	375	375	375	375	4,500
Sundries	100	100	100	100	100	100	100	100	100	100	100	100	1,200
BAS			2000			2000			2000			2000	8,000
Drawings	3000	3000	3000	3000	3000	3000	3000	3000	3000	3000	3000	3000	36,000
Total	4,075	4,075	6,075	4,075	4,075	6,075	4,075	4,075	6,075	4,075	4,075	6,075	56,900
Net cash flow	875	875	−1,125	875	875	−1,125	875	875	−1,125	875	875	−1,125	2,500
Cash position	875	1,750	625	1,500	2,375	1,250	2,125	3,000	1,875	2,750	3,625	2,500	

Summary

Shifts in customer behaviour resulting from the pandemic mean that old ways of doing business have given way to new concerns about health and safety, a rapid uptake of digitalisation, and a renewed emphasis on buying locally. With this in mind, we are looking for product ideas, service ideas, market ideas, and maybe even a radical idea. Not all ideas are good ideas, however, so a method for assessing ideas for their commercial potential is presented. Whether you are starting from scratch, buying an existing business, or buying a franchise, a practical blueprint significantly improves your prospects for success. It is the key to making a smooth transition from your initial idea to a going concern. It identifies your target market and your plans for making sales, the day-to-day procedures for operating the business, the financial results you expect to achieve, and a checklist of the things you need to do to get started.

2 Start-up essentials

The procedures for starting a business are governed by a variety of laws and regulations. They include creating a legal structure, applying for an Australian Business Number (ABN), registering a name, applying for a Tax File Number (TFN), getting any necessary licences and permits, finding premises if you need them, and making sure you are properly insured against business risks. If you decide to engage staff, then you will also need to know your obligations as an employer.

Legal structure

One of your first decisions is whether to set up your business as a sole proprietor, a partnership, a proprietary company, or a trust.

Sole proprietorship

A sole proprietorship is the easiest and simplest legal form in which a business can be organised. Because of its simplicity, it is the least expensive form to organise. The proprietor is the one and only owner of the business and has complete control over it. As sole owner of the business, the proprietor is also personally liable for business debts. A sole proprietorship is automatically terminated by the death or incapacity of the owner.

Advantages	Disadvantages
Low start-up costs	Ease of formation
More freedom from regulation	Unlimited personal liability
Owner is in direct control	Narrow management base
All profits go to the owner	Lack of continuity
Maximum privacy	Difficulty in raising capital
Easy to change legal structure	

Partnership

A partnership is the conduct of a business by two or more people who have the status and authority of owners or principals. Most partnerships are based on an

DOI: 10.4324/9781003394808-4

agreement or contract among the co-owners. Nevertheless, a formal contract is not essential because a partnership comes into existence when two or more people begin conducting business together for profit.

The law does not regard the partnership itself as a legal entity. Legally, it is simply two or more individuals. The assets of the business are viewed as belonging to the partners, and they are personally responsible for its debts. Each partner is an agent of the business and of the partners. Therefore, even a partner who is not particularly experienced or skilled in business affairs has the power to enter into contracts or other transactions that are binding on the other partners.

Advantages	Disadvantages
Ease of formation	Unlimited personal liability
Low start-up costs	Lack of continuity
More sources of capital	Divided authority
Broader management base	Possible friction between partners
Privacy of affairs	Less flexibility in transferring
Limited outside regulation	ownership interests
	Easy to change legal structure

There are also provisions for a *limited partnership*. This form of partnership enables some partners to contribute capital while retaining limited liability for the debts and obligations of the partnership.

Proprietary company

A company is recognised in law as having an existence separate and apart from its owner(s). The company holds property, enters into contracts, transfers property, and conducts legal matters in a capacity separate and distinct from its owner(s). The company is also recognised as a separate entity for tax purposes. There are provisions for a *single person company*, which only needs one director and one shareholder who can be the same individual.

Advantages

- Your liability on business obligations, and therefore your risk, is limited to the amount you pay for your shares.
- The company has a continuous existence, which means that it is not dissolved by the death, insanity, or withdrawal of an owner.
- An interest in the business represented by shares can be bought or sold, thus enabling you to withdraw from the company without jeopardising its continuity.

Disadvantages

- There is less privacy and closer regulation by the government and the courts.
- It is more expensive to organise and maintain.
- You may be restricted in what you can do by your company's constitution.
- Extra reporting requirements necessitate more record-keeping.
- Director's duties impose added personal responsibility.

The requirements for forming and operating a proprietary company are set down in the Corporations Law, which is administered by the Australian Securities and Investments Commission (ASIC). They are responsible for ensuring that company directors and officers carry out their duties honestly, diligently, and in the best interests of the company. The ASIC registers all companies and ensures that information about them is publicly available. You can visit the ASIC website at *asic.gov.au*.

The duties of a company director are complex, so make sure you know what you are getting yourself into. The Australian Institute of Company Directors (AICD) is the professional organisation for company directors in Australia. It provides leadership on company director issues, promotes excellence in corporate governance, provides company director education and development programmes, and publishes *Company Director* magazine. The national office is in Sydney, and there are offices in each state capital and the ACT. If you intend to become a company director, then joining the AICD can help you prepare for the role. You can visit their website at *aicd.companydirectors.com.au*.

Trust

Some businesses are organised as a *discretionary trust*. A trust is not a legal entity. It simply holds property in trust for the beneficiaries. The trustee administers the trust in accordance with the trust deed, which may give the trustee wide discretionary powers over the distribution of trust income and capital. Many of the advantages of a company can be maintained by having the company act as the trustee. For example, this enables the members of a family business to retain control over the trust by becoming directors of the Trustee Company as well as beneficiaries of the trust.

Advantages	Disadvantages
Flexibility	Costly to set up and run
Continuity can be preserved	Complicated to administer
Limited liability is possible	Limited life of the trust deed
More privacy than a company	Trustee is subject to the Trustee Act
Potential tax advantages	Powers restricted to the trust deed

An alternative arrangement is a *unit trust*, in which the beneficial ownership of the trust property is divided into units. Unit trusts differ from discretionary trusts in that trust property is divided on a predetermined basis according to the number of units held. There is no discretion to vary the proportional distribution of income and capital. Beneficiaries of the unit trust may act as the trustees and the units may be bought and sold, making it possible for individuals to withdraw from the business by selling their units.

Australian Business Number

The ABN is a unique 11-digit number that identifies a business. For example, you generally need to put your ABN on your invoices and other documents relating to sales. You also need an ABN in certain dealings with the Tax Office and other areas of government. You can apply for an ABN online through the Australian Business Register at *abr.gov.au*.

Having an ABN is not compulsory, but you will need one for things like registering for the GST, confirming your business identity to others when ordering and invoicing, avoiding PAYG withholding tax on payments you receive, and applying for an Australian domain name for your website. Also, some businesses and government departments will only deal with you if you have an ABN because it is regarded as evidence that you are a genuine business. If you choose a company structure, the ASIC will issue your company a nine-digit Australian Company Number (ACN). When you register your company for an ABN, you will be asked for your ACN. The ABN issued to your company by the Australian Business Register will be the company's ACN plus two extra digits.

Registering a name

Choosing a name for your business is important not only commercially but also legally. There are several types of names, and it is important to understand the differences between them because a *name* can be a company name, a business name, a domain name, or a trademark. It is essential to register your name in every category if you want to be sure that your business identity is protected.

Choosing a name

Choosing a name for your business takes some thought. Look for a name that reinforces your image and communicates the nature of your business clearly. Your name is a valuable asset, so it is worth the time and effort to get it right. Here are some tips that may help.

- Is the name meaningful? Your business name is the first thing most customers will know about your business. Make certain it focuses on your business image and avoid any name that is vague about what you do.

- Is the name easy to understand and pronounce? The key is to have a short business name that is easy to recall and less likely to be confused. This is particularly important if you are going to rely on word-of-mouth recommendations.
- Does the name have longevity? Think ahead about how your business might evolve and pick a name that is not only broad enough to give you room to grow but also narrow enough to retain the power to communicate its focus.
- Is the name unique? It needs to be clearly differentiated from other names. Have a list of three or four alternate names in case your first choice is already taken.
- Try out some possibilities with your family and friends. It is enlightening to see how other people react to a proposed business name.

Company name

A company name must be registered in accordance with the Corporations Law, which is administered by the ASIC. The name of a proprietary company must contain the words *Proprietary Limited* or its abbreviation *Pty Ltd*. If a company trades under a name other than its registered company name, then the trading name must also be registered as a business name.

Business name

Any person who carries on a business that does not consist of their surname and all given names (or the initials) needs to register a business name before the business can trade. The ASIC is responsible for registering, renewing, and administering business names. To register, update or search business name details, go to the ASIC website at *asic.gov.au*.

The reason for requiring the registration of a business name is to enable the public to find out who is operating under a business name. It also serves to avoid confusion by ensuring that no two businesses are registered under the same or similar names. When you register your business name, you will need to provide your ABN, personal details, an email address, a residential address, and an address for the service of documents. When your business name is approved and registered, it must appear on every business letter, invoice, and receipt.

Domain name

Your domain name is your website address on the Internet, and it gives you an online identity or brand. It's a valuable part of your business image and an important marketing tool that helps customers find and identify your business. If you want to register a *.com.au* or *.net.au* Internet address you will need to be a commercial entity and have either an Australian Company Number (ACN) or ABN. If you don't have a website, you can still register a domain name for use later. To register a domain name, go to the. au Domain Administration Ltd. website at *auda.org.au* for links to registrars and resellers.

Trademark

A trademark is a letter, word, phrase, sound, smell, colour, shape, logo, picture, aspect of packaging, or any combination of these things that identifies your product or service and distinguishes it from similar products and services. The owner of a trademark has exclusive legal rights to control the use of the trademark for the goods and services for which it is registered. Trademark registration is administered by IP Australia, and you can visit their website at *ipaustralia.gov.au*.

Tax File Number

A TFN is required by the Australian Taxation Office (ATO) to identify each taxpayer. If you decide to operate your business as a sole proprietor, then you will use your individual TFN for both your personal and business dealings with the ATO. You can apply for a personal TFN at Australia Post, through Centrelink, or by downloading the form from the ATO website at *ato.gov.au*. If you decide to operate your business as a partnership, company, or trust, then you will need a separate TFN. Partnerships, companies, and trusts can apply for a TFN online via the Australian Business Register website at *abr.gov.au.*

Australian Business Licence Information Service

Most businesses require one or more licences and/or permits before they can begin operating. Licences regulate activities, locations, events, services, equipment, premises, operators, and occupations. In addition to licences that apply to specific types of businesses or occupations, there are other licences that apply to all businesses. This can be a perplexing problem because licences may be required by a variety of Commonwealth, state, and local government authorities. Your first stop should be the Australian Business Licence Information Service (ABLIS) website at *ablis.business.gov.au*. ABLIS provides one-stop advice about licences, permits, approvals, and registrations. Their website not only identifies which licences a business requires but also provides a package containing information and application forms. This is an important service because it dramatically reduces wasted time and frustration.

Premises

For businesses that are just starting out, finding premises is usually driven by necessity. The choice of premises includes working from home, renting a serviced office, joining a business incubator, or setting up commercial premises.

Working from home

Going to work once meant travelling from home to a factory, shop, or office. A revolution in the way many Australians go to work has led to an enormous increase in the number of home-based businesses, especially as a result of the pandemic. Garages and spare bedrooms are being transformed into the new workplace. About 70 per cent operate *at* home and the remaining 30 per cent operate *from* home.

Many start-ups are attracted to working at home because of family and life-style considerations. The hours lost commuting, the long working hours, and the stress of abandoning young children to day-care centres have prompted some individuals to review their career aspirations and what they want out of life. They can have an office at home with no overheads, they can be close at hand for the family, and their working hours can be as flexible as they like. Technology is perhaps the most powerful force behind the growth of home-based businesses. Relatively inexpensive and powerful computers, email, mobile phones, and the Internet have helped to make the home-based business functionally and financially feasible.

There are also a few pitfalls to consider if you want to work from home. Be sure the local council approves the use of residential premises for business pur-poses. You could find yourself in violation of zoning regulations. Ensure that your business activities don't attract complaints from your neighbours because of traffic, parking, noise, pollution, or other reasons. Make sure you have enough space to operate satisfactorily without intruding on other members of the house-hold. You can obtain tax benefits from your home-based business, but this can also lead to a loss of part of your tax-free capital gain when you sell your home. It is easy to succumb to the inevitable distractions and interruptions when you work at home, so you will need a measure of self-discipline in order to establish an effective working routine. And last, working at home can be a lonely lifestyle if you are accustomed to the social interaction of a workplace.

Serviced office

An alternative to setting up a home office is to rent space in a serviced office. Serviced office complexes can provide furnishings, IT services, telephone answering services, word processing services, photocopying, fax, postal, and courier services. They typically have a reception area and meeting rooms. Sec-retarial staff are generally available on a casual basis. The major advantage is that you only pay for what you need and you don't pay for unused space or idle staff when business is quiet. When things get busy, however, you have extra capacity at your fingertips.

Business incubator

Business incubators are usually targeted towards the needs of firms engaged in light manufacturing, services, or research and development. They are seldom suitable for retail businesses. Incubators offer office and factory space with on-site expert advice. The idea is to provide an environment in which a new business can achieve self-sufficiency before becoming independent and moving to other premises. Like a serviced office, you can rent the space you need for a short period and you only pay for the services you use. You are not locked into a long-term lease, and you have access to guidance and advice. Most business incubators are sponsored by government or non-profit organisations. Some are affiliated with universities to commercialise technical innovations. A few are joint ventures with private investment groups. Business incubators vary tremendously in the services they offer and the fees they charge.

Setting up commercial premises

If you want to set up a shop or a factory, it will need to be registered under state and local government jurisdictions. These requirements vary enormously from one location to another, and they involve a number of different government departments. You can save yourself a lot of confusion by first consulting with your state small business agency and the ABLIS website to determine exactly which regulations apply to your premises.

Although many regulations are enforced through state government departments, you will need to pay particular attention to local government zoning and the use of buildings. When you occupy premises, you need to ensure that you conform to the council's planning scheme. Make an appointment to discuss your proposal with the council's planning staff. Any change in the use of a building or land will require an application to the council for its consent. If there are no building works, you can begin trading within the limits and subject to the conditions specified by the council in its consent. If any alterations, additions, or new building works are proposed, then a building application will also be required. It is wise to discuss the council's building requirements in advance with both the building inspector and the health inspector.

Insurance

You should consider insurance protection against certain types of potential losses. Insurance *brokers* are independent of the insurance companies, and it is their job to shop around for the most suitable policies, provide you with advice, arrange the paperwork, and assist with claims.

Public risk insurance

Public risk insurance covers injuries to others while they are on your premises. Failure to recognise the dangers of not carrying public risk insurance can be a serious mistake because one big claim can wipe you out. Some public risks are not covered by public risk policies and need to be insured separately, such as third-party motor vehicle insurance, product liability insurance, and workers' compensation insurance.

Fire and property insurance

The term *fire insurance* has a much wider meaning than simply insuring property against damage caused by fire or lightning. Other risks that can be covered by a fire policy include damage caused by:

Aircraft	Water
Explosions	Flood
Riots, strikes, and vandalism	Storm and tempest
Impact by vehicles, horses, or cattle	Earthquake Electric current (fusion)

The most convenient way to buy fire insurance is to combine all of your coverage under one policy. You are less likely to duplicate coverage, settlement of claims is easier, and the total premium is usually lower. If you are running a business from home, be aware that home and contents policies don't normally cover business losses.

Business continuation insurance

If your business is shut down as a result of a fire or flood, you may be protected for the loss of property, but not for the loss of cash flow to pay the bills while you rebuild. Similarly, if a partner dies, you may not be able to keep operating without their skills. *Business interruption insurance*, sometimes called *consequential loss insurance*, is usually an addition to your fire insurance policy that reimburses you for part of the lost profit and a portion of your fixed costs while you are out of action. *Partnership insurance* provides cash to keep a partnership business intact in the event of the death of one of the partners. Since the death of a partner legally ends a partnership, the proceeds of this insurance can be used by the surviving partner to buy the deceased partner's interest from their estate. *Key person insurance* is the same as partnership insurance, except the beneficiary is the business itself.

Insuring a home-based business

It is a big mistake to rely on a standard homeowner's insurance policy to cover a home-based business. It means that the repair shop in your garage, the merchandise that you keep stored in the spare room, or the computer equipment in your home office may not be covered. Moreover, even though you are covered for injury to a visiting guest, your homeowner's policy may not cover injury to individuals who are at your home on business.

There are three ways to make sure your home-based business is properly covered. You can broaden your existing homeowner's policy by asking your insurer to include *endorsements* to cover specific business risks. You can buy an explicit home-based business endorsement offered by some insurers. Or you can buy standard commercial insurance called a *Business Owner's Policy*.

Employing staff

It is one thing to be self-employed, but it is quite another thing to become an employer. As an employer, you are faced with an array of Commonwealth and state or territory legislation including the Fair Work Act, anti-discrimination legislation, superannuation legislation, long service leave legislation, occupational health and safety legislation, workers' compensation legislation, and taxation legislation. Perhaps this explains why more than half of the small businesses in Australia don't employ staff. Before you contemplate engaging staff, make sure you understand how much time, effort, and expense goes into being an employer. Eventually, you may find that you cannot do everything yourself and you will need to employ staff. From this point on, the greatest asset in your business will be the people who work for you.

Fair work system

The Fair Work System is Australia's national workplace relations system. It has changed the arrangements for regulating Australia's workplace law and made it easier to navigate the legal labyrinth of employment law. The Fair Work website at *fairwork.gov.au* is a comprehensive source of information about current employment legislation and regulation.

The Fair Work System is underpinned by the National Employment Standards. The Standards provide a set of minimum conditions for all employees covered by the national workplace relations system. The Standards set out such things as maximum hours of work, leave, and redundancy pay entitlements. Neither an award nor an enterprise bargaining agreement can be used to get around the Standards. Information about the Standards is available on the Fair Work website.

For some types of jobs or for employees of certain types of businesses, there is an award that sets out the minimum conditions for that kind of work. Awards may include conditions such as rates of pay, penalty rates and allowances, hours of work, and leave entitlements. Visit the Fair Work website to find out if an award applies to your business.

Enterprise agreements are arrangements for pay and conditions that are negotiated between an employer and employees, and they override an award that would otherwise apply. Enterprise agreements are different from awards because they can cover a broader range of matters and they can be tailored to a particular business's needs. However, enterprise agreements cannot remove the safety net conditions contained in the Standards. In order to make an agreement, the parties must bargain with each other in good faith, genuinely agree to the conditions, and lodge the agreement with Fair Work Australia for approval. For more information, visit the Fair Work website.

Occupational health and safety

Workplace safety means you are required to identify and manage risks in the workplace. For particular industries and certain types of jobs, there are codes of practice for how certain risks are to be managed. If there are no guidelines for a particular job or task, you are nevertheless required to take reasonable precautions and exercise due care. Some activities are considered highly risky and require specific training, licences, and permits for employees involved in or overseeing these jobs. Each State retains its own workplace safety authority with inspectors who visit workplaces and investigate incidents. For more information, visit the Safe Work Australia website at *safeworkaustralia.gov.au*.

Workers' compensation insurance

Employers are required to have workers' compensation insurance for their employees. In the event of a work-related injury or disease, there is an entitlement to claim for a range of medical costs and income support. The level of risk associated with a particular industry, an employer's track record of providing a safe workplace, and the amount of wages paid to workers determine the premiums that are paid. For information on insurance requirements, policy providers, and claims procedures, see your state or territory small business agency website.

Summary

Starting a business involves a number of initial requirements, and you may need professional advice for some of them. First, decide if you want to operate as a sole trader, a partnership, a company, or under a trust arrangement. Next, register your legal entity and trading name, your ABN, and your TFN. Check with the ABLIS to see what other licences or permits you need before you begin operating. Find out what you need to do if you will be working from home, renting office space, joining an incubator, or setting up your own shop or factory. Make sure you insure yourself against potential losses from things like fire, theft, burglary, and accidents. If you are going to employ staff, take some time to learn about your responsibilities as an employer.

3 Getting help

Much anxiety and worry can be avoided, especially in the early stages, if you take advantage of the help and assistance that is available. These include professional advisers, specialist consultants, locally based support organisations, state and territory small business agencies, and a number of Commonwealth government agencies and departments.

Professional advisers

Initially, your professional advisers will be a solicitor and an accountant. Later, you may want specialist advice in other areas. Make sure your advisers know what you expect of them and what results you want to achieve. If they don't deliver the goods, don't be afraid to replace them. At the same time, remember that good advice costs money, so be prepared to pay for the best advice you can get. A professional adviser may be an individual, a local firm, or part of a national or international organisation. The big firms are not generally interested in servicing small clients, and their fees are usually expensive. Instead, look locally for professional advisers that offer ready access to an experienced partner.

Legal advice

Most solicitors are skilled in the legal mechanics of business, and they can save you a great deal of time and frustration. Look for a solicitor that has training and experience in commercial law and is familiar with the problems of small business operators. Take them into your confidence and keep them informed of any matters with possible legal implications. A solicitor should be able to provide you with a range of legal services, including:

Registration procedures	Conveyancing
Leases	Warranties
Legal organisation	Litigation
Partnership agreements	Liabilities and insurance
Contracts	Effects of legislation
Employment agreements	Winding up

DOI: 10.4324/9781003394808-5

Financial advice

Make sure you are talking to a Chartered Accountant (CA), a Certified Practising Accountant (CPA) or a member of the Institute of Public Accountants (IPA). Experience has shown that most small businesses only use their accountant for the preparation of tax returns and statutory reports. However, accountants can provide a range of services including:

Taxation advice	Financial statements
Auditing	Purchase/sale of a business
Planning and budgeting	Information systems
Preparing loan applications	Statutory reports and returns
Bookkeeping	Cash flow analysis
Investment advice	Superannuation planning
Payroll services	Cost analysis.

Specialist advice

If you run into a tough problem that you cannot handle by yourself, then it may be time to engage a consultant. Consultants can help with a variety of assignments.

Digital technology	**Production**
Domain name	Methods
Website	Layout
Hosting service	Standards
Payment systems	Quality control
Mobile methods	Cost

Management	**Marketing**
Recruiting	Digital marketing
Training	Advertising
Industrial relations	Packaging
Compensation	Distribution
Motivation	Point-of-sale

A consultant needs an accurate *brief* that describes the nature of the work you want done. Be sure the consultant you choose is a specialist in the field, dedicated to the problem at hand, and only retained for as long as it takes to complete the assignment. Ask for a firm estimate of their fees and expenses and get references from past clients before you offer them an assignment. They should give you regular reports on their progress, and at the completion of the assignment, they should discuss the results with you and provide a comprehensive report.

Local support

There is typically a range of experience, skills, and resources available in your local community. These include business mentors, your nearest Business Enterprise Centre (BEC), and the trade association for your kind of business.

Business mentor

A business mentor is someone with experience and knowledge who can advise and guide you on a range of business matters. Business mentors are coaches, not consultants, nor do they take the place of your accountant or your solicitor. Instead, it's a relationship between you and a trusted individual with business experience who can guide you through making decisions, point out ways of improving your operation, ask you the tough questions, and encourage you to achieve your goals.

A business mentor is typically motivated by a desire to foster the development of individuals who want to go into business. They generally do so voluntarily. There are no risks in working with a business mentor. No one is going to tell you what to do or how to run your business. The objective of working with a business mentor is to gain fresh insights into your business through impartial, objective discussion and feedback. There are various ways in which you could benefit from working with a business mentor.

- Exploring options becomes easier when you have the counsel of someone who understands and shares your concerns.
- Having someone to motivate you and help you concentrate your attention on the things that matter most.
- By focusing your time and energy, you may be able to achieve your goals more quickly.
- A business mentor may be able to point out business opportunities that you have missed.
- A business mentor can help you step back from your business to identify strengths, weaknesses, opportunities, and threats.
- A growing business brings new challenges such as hiring staff, raising capital, and entering new markets. A business mentor can offer advice about best practice, caution against potential pitfalls, and help you have confidence in your plans.
- The key role of a business mentor is to listen, stimulate, and challenge your thinking. This will help you to develop ideas and arrive at solutions more quickly than doing it on your own.
- A business mentor can help you establish your business network by introducing you to people within your industry as well as other professionals.

Locating a business mentor will take some digging. Do you know anyone with the right skills and experience that you could ask to be your mentor? Your state or territory government small business agency and your nearest BEC have mentor matching programmes that will help you find a business mentor. Your accountant and solicitor may also be able to help.

Business enterprise centre

A BEC is a community-based business assistance organisation. Through their partnership with Commonwealth and State governments, private enterprise, and local communities across Australia, BECs provide practical, confidential business facilitation services. There are BEC offices throughout Australia. To find out how you can benefit from your nearest BEC, visit their website at *becaustralia.org.au*. A BEC understands local issues, so they are capable of providing the kind of assistance that is relevant in your local community. If the expertise you need is not available at your local BEC, they can call upon colleagues in other BECs to help. BEC business advisory services include:

- Literature and publications on topics such as taxation, business registration, marketing, and business benchmarks.
- Training programmes on topics such as:

  o Starting a business   o Business compliance
  o Financial management   o Business planning
  o Record keeping   o Customer service
  o Marketing   o Social media for business
  o Management skills

- BECs have a network of local professionals they can refer you to, such as accountants, solicitors, marketing consultants, insurers, and tax consultants.
- There are government grants and assistance programmes that you can discuss with your BEC Business Advisor.
- BECs encourage local businesses to meet with each other, share experiences, and develop strategic alliances.
- Business mentoring support can be arranged through your nearest BEC.
- A BEC can assist you with business feasibility testing, business planning, and advice on buying a business.

Trade association

A trade association consists of people who are engaged in the same or similar types of businesses. These organisations tend to be the best source of industry-specific information and assistance. When you find the right trade association, join it and take advantage of all the information and assistance that it provides. Most trade associations hold regular meetings where you can meet with others in the trade to discuss matters of common interest. Services that may be available from a trade association include:

- Information and publications
- Computer systems
- Benchmarking and industry profiles
- Advice and/or advocacy on industrial relations matters
- Advice on legislation and government regulations

- Taxation advice
- Insurance advice
- Joint advertising and promotion of industry products
- Publicity and public relations
- Seminars, lectures, and workshops
- Referrals to specialist advisers and consultants.

State and territory support

Each state and territory government operates a small business agency. The services vary, but they usually include:

On-line resources	Business licensing
Publications	Referrals
Training programmes	Financial assistance
Counselling and advice	

You can find information about your state or territory small business agency by visiting their website.

ACT	*business.act.gov.au*
NSW	*smallbusiness.nsw.gov.au*
NT	*nt.gov.au/industry*
QLD	*business.qld.gov.au*
SA	*business.sa.gov.au*
TAS	*business.tas.gov.au*
VIC	*business.vic.gov.au*
WA	*smallbusiness.wa.gov.au*

Commonwealth support

Over the years, there have been scores of Commonwealth government small business programmes. It is incredibly difficult to keep tabs on the vast number of programmes as they ebb and flow with the political and economic tide. This has been particularly true in the wake of the pandemic crisis. The best way to find your way around the labyrinth of Commonwealth government programmes is to visit the website at ***business.gov.au*** where you will find the most comprehensive directory in Australia for small business tools, resources, information, and assistance.

Summary

Going into business for yourself does not mean you are completely on your own. Professional advice is available from your solicitor, your accountant, and specialist consultants. A business mentor can give you the benefit of their knowledge and experience. The nearest BEC and your trade association will also be able to provide advisory services. State and territory government small business agencies and various Commonwealth government departments and agencies have a range of assistance programmes that you can access by visiting their websites.

Part A

Reality check

What are the risks?

The purpose of these questions is to identify and evaluate the risks associated with commercialising an idea. There are a number of potential risks in the early stages of a start-up, and we distinguish between those that are outside the business and those that are inside the business. External risks are generally beyond your control but may nevertheless restrict the commercial potential of an idea. Internal risks are related to the way a start-up is organised and there is more you can do to manage them. Potential risks are evaluated by answering a series of questions. By selecting the answers that best describe your idea, you will be able to judge if you think the risks are acceptable. The answers will also become part of the Commercial Feasibility Rating in the Appendix.

External risks

External risks restrict the commercial potential of an idea because they limit the ways in which it can be exploited. These risks are often beyond our control.

- Compliance risk not only is concerned with the law but also includes other forms of regulation and standards.
- Technology risk is the way in which technological change may challenge the competitive position of an idea.
- Economic risk consists of changes in the economy that affect the commercial outlook for an idea.
- Political risk refers to changes in government policy that may alter the commercial potential of an idea.
- Dependence risk refers to a limitation on an idea because it depends on another product or service or needs the support of a gatekeeper.

There is little that can be done to change the nature of external risks, but it is possible to position a business to minimise their effect. The task is to recognise which external risks apply to an idea and decide if you are prepared to live with them.

DOI: 10.4324/9781003394808-6

Compliance risk

Compliance risk covers nearly every aspect of business, including competition, financial transactions, health, safety, the environment, and more. Compliance includes not only legal restrictions imposed at Commonwealth, state, and local government levels but also regulation by government agencies, non-government agencies, and industry associations. The risks from regulation are increasing, particularly with the trend towards a more intrusive, more comprehensive, and more prescriptive approach by regulators. Laws and regulations made by the government and other regulatory bodies can significantly increase the cost of operating a business, reduce the attractiveness of making an investment, or change the market potential of an idea. Sometimes it is simply not worth the cost or the effort. The following list is a sample of regulatory websites.

- Australian Securities and Investments Commission at *asic.gov.au*
- Fair Work Ombudsman at *fairwork.gov.au*
- Department of Agriculture, Water and the Environment at *environment. gov.au*
- IP Australia at *ipaustralia.gov.au*
- Australian Trade and Investment Commission at *austrade.gov.au*
- Australian Border Force at *abf.gov.au*
- Safe Work Australia at *safeworkaustralia.gov.au*
- Australian Taxation Office at *ato.gov.au*
- Australian Prudential Regulation Authority at *apra.gov.au*
- Standards Australia at *standards.org.au*
- Australian Competition and Consumer Commission at *accc.gov.au*

1. In terms of the relevant laws, standards, and other regulations, will my idea . . .

   a) meet them without any changes?
   b) require only minor changes?
   c) require moderate changes?
   d) require substantial changes?
   e) probably not meet them at all?

Technology risk

Technology is the basis for many new business opportunities, but it also represents a significant source of risk. Technological change makes existing products and services obsolete, and new technology inevitably destroys the market for inferior technology. The greatest risk of technological disruption occurs when a market is mature and saturated. For example, when personal computers capable of word processing burst onto the scene, the market for typewriters collapsed. A related risk is the way in which technological change can shorten the commercial lifespan of ideas.

For some ideas, it is the technology itself that is the curse. Many high-tech ideas fail because the developer falls in love with the technology and ignores the market that it is intended to serve. They mistakenly assume that customers will find their new technology as enticing and irresistible as they do. Recognising changes in technology is the easy part. Predicting the forces that will actually drive people to use it is the difficult part. Customers are interested in how an idea meets their needs, not the technological brilliance that produced it, and they will not pay for technology that they don't need just because it is offered.

Perhaps the biggest technological risk for every business is failing to embrace technology in the face of competitive pressure from businesses that do. Broadband and wireless networks have become widespread. More advanced and cheaper computer power is making it easier to collect, analyse, and share information. The Internet is a platform for providing new tools, services, and resources. Technology is going to be cheaper and simpler to use, and it will play a role in almost every business idea.

2. Will the technology on which my idea is based be . . .

    a)   very stable for the foreseeable future?
    b)   reasonably stable for the foreseeable future?
    c)   subject to some disruptive developments?
    d)   subject to significant disruptive developments?
    e)   likely to be replaced by new technology very soon?

Economic risk

The business cycle consists of periods of economic expansion and contraction. Expansionary phases are characterised by more jobs, higher incomes, and increased spending. If the economy grows too quickly, however, then inflation rises and purchasing power declines in real terms. A slowdown in spending and the resulting economic contraction sometimes lead to a period of recession. The three main economic risks are consumer and business confidence, inflation, and interest rates.

Consumer and business confidence drive economic activity. The more confident people are, the more they will spend and the greater will be economic activity. When they lose confidence, they curtail their spending and economic activity slows down. Changes in consumer and business confidence are driven by things that affect their purchasing power, including taxation, economic growth, employment, inflation, interest rates, government spending, exchange rates, and the stage of the business cycle.

When inflation stays at an acceptable level, prices remain stable, and consumers and businesses are more likely to be confident. The goal of the Reserve Bank of Australia is to try to keep the average inflation rate around 2 to 3 per cent over the course of the business cycle. When demand is high, prices will rise unless there is a corresponding increase in supply. Higher prices mean getting less for the same number of dollars, so consumers and businesses will be unable to sustain their purchasing in real terms without going into debt.

Changes in the level of interest rates affect how much consumers and businesses are prepared to borrow. Similarly, an increase in interest rates affects firms' willingness to borrow money for new investments. While interest rates were at historical lows for a long time, they have gone up recently along with the rate of inflation.

3.   Will the near-term outlook for the economy be . . .

    a)   very positive for my idea?
    b)   reasonably positive for my idea?
    c)   neutral for my idea?
    d)   somewhat negative for my idea?
    e)   very negative for my idea?

Political risk

Proposed changes in government policy can alter the feasibility of an idea. These include policy decisions about taxes, spending, regulation, exchange rates, trade tariffs, industrial relations, and environmental regulations. Political risk includes policies not only at the Commonwealth government level but also at the state and local government levels.

When the government decides to change a policy, it alters the risk/reward trade-off for those ideas that are affected. Subsidies create an incentive for new commercial opportunities, whereas extra taxes are more likely to create a disincentive. For instance, if the government spends more on research for renewable energy, it increases the income potential for ideas that embrace the new technology. On the other hand, if the government increases taxes on renewable energy, it will have the same effect as an increase in costs.

Policy decisions in other countries also create political risks. When the United Kingdom voted to leave the European Union (Brexit), it not only caused commercial disruption across Europe but also injected uncertainty about trading arrangements with other countries including Australia. In the United States, former President Trump's changes to major regulations, trade relations, tariffs, healthcare, work visas, and taxes created unprecedented disruption not only to existing commercial relationships but also to the potential for some ideas in Australia.

4.   Will the extent to which my idea might be at risk from current or proposed government policy be . . .

    a)   very low?
    b)   low?
    c)   moderate?
    d)   high?
    e)   very high?

Dependence risk

Dependence occurs when an idea must rely on some other product, process, service, system, person, or organisation to make sales. For example, manufacturers of printers depend largely on the sales of personal computers and the retailers who recommend which printer to buy. Any change in the sales of personal computers or the recommendations of resellers will have a knock-on effect that the printer manufacturers cannot control. If dependence risk is low, then you have greater control over your marketing strategy and more scope to exploit an idea. If dependence risk is high, you need to look for ways to resist it. For example, you could approach the seller of a product on which you are dependent about forming a strategic alliance in which you bundle your products together.

Gatekeepers are a special category of dependence risk. They can decide things like what should be produced, what should be sold, how it should be sold, what customers should buy, and sometimes who has the right to be a customer. Fortunately, traditional gatekeeping systems are going through a period of decline. The end of intermediaries and the shortening of distribution channels enable more sellers to go directly to their customers.

5. Will the dependence of my idea on another product, process, service, system, person, or organisation be . . .

    a) very low?
    b) low?
    c) moderate?
    d) high?
    e) very high?

Internal risks

Internal risks result from flaws in the way in which an idea is commercialised, so it is important to know what they might be and what you can do about them. Keep in mind that risk is relative, and decisions about what kinds of risks you may be willing to take need to be made with the possible rewards in mind.

*   Planning risk refers to inadequate preparation for commercialising an idea.
*   Marketing risk refers to target market information that is not accurate or complete.
*   Deliverable's risk refers to the uncertainty that an idea may not be able to be delivered at an acceptable standard.
*   Liquidity risk refers to not having enough cash to sustain the start-up process.
*   Personal risk refers to the stress and uncertainty involved in commercialising an idea and the potential impact on your personal life.

Planning risk

Planning risk means not having a blueprint for making the transition from your initial idea to a going concern. Planning significantly increases the chances for success. It helps to prevent viewing the future in ways that the facts don't support, and it exposes problems early before they become an unexpected crisis. Planning cannot predict change, but it helps to recognise it and construct a strategy accordingly.

Planning is not a guarantee of success, but research has shown that the chances of succeeding increase with the frequency and quality of planning. Stick to a short planning period of one or two years and go for a rolling plan that can be regularly reviewed and updated. Write it down, but don't make it long or complicated.

6.   Has a blueprint for commercialising my idea been . . .

    a)   completely finished?
    b)   substantially finished?
    c)   started, but there is much to do?
    d)   put off, but it is intended to do one?
    e)   unnecessary because it is all in my head?

Marketing risk

Marketing risk means not fully understanding the characteristics of the target market and how it can be captured. Without customers, there is no commercial potential, and without satisfying a genuine need or want, there will be no customers. The risk is that you may not have enough information that is accurate and complete. The goal is to know how you are going to deliver exactly the right benefits to the best market segment(s) you can target.

Market information is important in choosing the right marketing strategy. An *undifferentiated* marketing strategy is one in which you target all market segments in the same way. This is a useful strategy for products and services for which there is a universal need, and it lends itself to mass marketing because there is little difference from one market segment to another. Alternatively, a *concentrated* marketing strategy is one in which you select just one market segment and specialise in being the best at meeting its needs. You are targeting fewer customers, but you are trying to capture a large proportion of them. A third marketing strategy is a *differentiated* marketing strategy, in which you have different marketing tactics for different market segments.

7.   Has the market research for my idea been . . .

    a)   completed and integrated into a marketing strategy?
    b)   completed but not yet integrated into a marketing strategy?
    c)   underway and will be finished soon?

d) put off for now, but it is intended to be done later?

e) unnecessary because it is all in my head?

Deliverable's risk

There are two parts to deliverable's risk. The first part relates to whether an idea will be fit for its intended purpose. For a product, we are interested in things like operating characteristics, features, flexibility, durability, conforming to standards, serviceability, aesthetics, and quality. For a service, we are interested in things like timeliness, courtesy, consistency, convenience, completeness, and accuracy. Ideas that face long or complicated research and development represent a greater risk that they may not be deliverable as originally envisaged.

The second part relates to the sequence of steps that will translate an idea into a tangible product or service. It includes not being able to bring together the skilled people, the right equipment, the right processes, and the right controls to deliver a consistent level of quality at an acceptable price. Some operations are simple and easily managed with standard operating procedures. Others are complex or vary considerably resulting in greater deliverable's risk.

Try to anticipate the deliverable's risks that are relevant to your idea and rate the likelihood that each could occur. Then consider the magnitude of the consequences for each one if it happens. Serious deliverable's risks in which countermeasures are unreliable or unavailable may be a reason to consider abandoning an idea.

8. Will I be able to deliver my idea . . .

a) consistently at a very high standard?

b) at a high standard most of the time?

c) at a high standard after further development?

d) at an acceptable standard after further development?

e) only after a significant research and development effort?

Liquidity risk

Liquidity risk means running out of money. Initially, money may be needed for research and development, market research, setting up distribution channels, training, equipment, premises, production, packaging, promotion, and working capital. The more money it takes to get the doors open, the greater the chance there will not be enough money to keep going until the business becomes cash positive. New businesses are especially vulnerable to liquidity problems because they tend to operate with inadequate cash reserves and miss the implications of a cash deficit until it is too late.

The liquidity cycle is a series of activities that continuously transform the components of working capital. Cash is transformed into raw materials by purchasing. Raw materials are transformed into finished goods by manufacturing.

Finished goods are transformed into accounts receivable by selling on credit. And accounts receivable are transformed back into cash when they are collected. The cycle repeats itself continuously so long as there are no bottlenecks to restrict its flow. When bottlenecks do occur, they cause a stop/start reaction that disrupts the liquidity cycle leading to a cash crisis.

The shorter the liquidity cycle, the less cash is required to be invested in the business, and the easier it is to maintain cash flow. The longer the liquidity cycle, the more cash is needed and the more difficult it is to maintain cash flow. If liquidity risk is a serious uncertainty, consider postponing a start-up until you have sufficient funds to get it underway.

9.   Will the liquidity cycle for my idea be . . .

   a)   a cash-only operation?
   b)   a short liquidity cycle?
   c)   a medium liquidity cycle?
   d)   a long liquidity cycle?
   e)   uncertain without further research?

Personal risk

It is one thing to recognise the commercial risks involved in an idea, but there are also personal risks that need to be considered. Commercialising an idea can create an enormous strain on your finances, your family, your social life, and your emotions. You will have to work long hours, which means time for family and friends will be difficult to find. Your income may become uncertain, and sometimes it could fluctuate enormously as a result of factors you cannot control. You will face the unrelenting pressure of solving problems when you are not sure about what to do.

The risk of failure is real, and the evidence tells us that it is greatest during the first year. If you fail, you will lose some money, maybe even all your money. You may feel bad for a while because your self-esteem will be bruised. There may even be some lingering ill will on the part of former partners, suppliers, employees, or customers.

There is also an element of luck, which means that success might elude you no matter how carefully you do your homework. You need to consider the personal risks involved in pursuing an idea and ask yourself if you are comfortable taking these risks. Not everyone shares the same attitude toward risk, so you need to be sure that your idea is within your comfort zone.

10. Will the personal risks involved in commercialising my idea be . . .

   a)   totally within my comfort zone?
   b)   reasonably within my comfort zone?
   c)   at the limit of my comfort zone?
   d)   outside my comfort zone?
   e)   well outside my comfort zone?

Feedback

The purpose of these questions is to identify and evaluate the potential risks associated with commercialising an idea. No evaluation system can fully anticipate all of the risks, yet this is precisely what needs to be done. For each of the questions, think about the response you have chosen, how it interacts with the other questions, and their collective impact on the overall risk of commercialising an idea. Good responses don't remove all of the risks involved, but they do suggest that the risks might be manageable. The responses for potential risks will also be incorporated into a Commercial Feasibility Rating in the Appendix.

External risks reflect conditions outside a business, and there is very little that can be done to change them. They may restrict the commercial potential of an idea because they limit the ways in which it can be exploited. The chapter examines compliance risk, technology risk, economic risk, political risk, and dependence risk in terms of selecting a response that best describes an idea you are evaluating. We are looking primarily for 'a' and 'b' responses. Those risks for which 'c' was selected throw up a question mark because there is little tolerance for external risks and 'c' responses need to be investigated further. Risks for which 'd' or 'e' was selected are likely to be unacceptable because they suggest fatal flaws in an idea's commercial potential.

Internal risks reflect conditions inside a business, and there is more scope to manage them. The diagnostic examines planning risk, marketing risk, deliverable's risk, liquidity risk, and personal risk in terms of selecting a response that best describes the idea you are evaluating. We are looking principally for 'a' and 'b' responses. Internal risks, for which 'c' was selected are tolerable but look for ways in which they can be minimised. Risks for which 'd' was selected are likely to be troublesome because they tend to become a persistent distraction. Risks for which 'e' was selected should be considered a red flag until they can be more accurately established.

Part B

Unlocking a marketing strategy

Marketing is a topic that is sometimes shrouded in mystery. Most business owners know that marketing is the most important element of their business, but they are not always sure where to begin or what strategies to use. The purpose of Part B is to show you how to create a marketing strategy and how traditional and digital marketing methods can be used to generate sales for your business.

Chapter 4 describes how to create a marketing strategy. It begins by gathering information about your customers so that you clearly understand what will influence their decision to buy from you. Having identified your market niche, the key is to put together a marketing mix that positions your business to attract customers like a magnet.

Chapter 5 explains a variety of traditional marketing methods. These include brochures and direct mail, newsletters, publicity, and sponsorship. It also includes various forms of paid advertising such as the Yellow Pages, classified and display ads in the newspaper, magazines, radio, television, and outdoor advertising. The chapter ends with an explanation of how to engage in personal selling.

Chapter 6 focuses on digital marketing methods. The acceptance and popularity of digital technology are more widespread than ever, resulting in an explosion of digital marketing opportunities. The chapter explains email marketing, social media platforms, online marketplaces, online directories, building your own website, online advertising, and marketing on mobile devices.

At the end of Part B, there is a reality check in which a series of questions are used to evaluate the strengths and weaknesses of an idea to capture its target market. Anticipated demand is an assessment of market size, market growth, market stability, commercial lifespan, and potential spinoffs. Market acceptance is an assessment of need, recognition, compatibility, complexity, and distribution. Market strength is an assessment of differentiation, value, customers, suppliers, and competitors. Combined, they provide an insight into the likelihood of an idea to capture its target market.

DOI: 10.4324/9781003394808-7

4 Marketing strategy

Marketing is the process of delivering benefits to customers who want to buy them. It consists of creating products and services that meet the needs and wants of customers, at a price they are willing to pay, and offered where and when they want to buy them. Marketing also consists of promotional methods such as advertising and sales that tell customers about the products and services on offer. Marketing is the lifeblood of every business, and it is the key to generating the revenue that pays the bills and makes a profit.

Marketing strategy is the way in which you design your marketing programme. It consists of understanding your customers' buying motives, dividing the market into segments with similar characteristics, selecting the best segment(s) to target, deciding how to position your product or service in the mind of your target market, and creating a marketing mix that delivers the benefits your customers want to buy. The purpose of this chapter is to consider each component of a marketing strategy and how to combine them to achieve the results you want.

Understanding customers

Understanding customers means identifying their buying motives. When they go shopping, they don't buy goods and services, they buy benefits. For example, when they decide to buy new tyres, some are buying safety, some are buying road handling performance while others are buying a sporty image. New and improved products and services regularly appear on the market, but customers' motives for buying them – such as health, beauty, safety, comfort, convenience, economy, and enjoyment – remain constant. Buying motives determine not only what customers buy but also how they buy. For example, what do you offer people who can only shop in the evenings or on weekends? You open at times that are convenient, thereby offering a benefit that appeals to one of their buying motives. A marketing strategy works best when it is squarely aimed at satisfying customers' buying motives, and the only things you should be selling are the benefits your customers want to buy.

You need information about customers that enables you to choose the right products and services to offer, the best ways to promote sales, the right prices

DOI: 10.4324/9781003394808-8

to charge, and the best way to deliver the goods. After your business is established, you will need more information to decide where to expand, where to cut back, or where to change emphasis. The better you understand your customers, the easier it is to create an effective marketing strategy. It is not simple, and it takes time, but knowing who your customers are, where they come from, what they like and dislike, and what benefits they want to buy will enable you to design a powerful marketing strategy. Being intuitive can sometimes work, but not for everyone and not all the time. Genuine research into understanding your customers is more likely to lead to accurate and useful information.

Finding a market niche

The first step in developing a marketing strategy is to find a market niche. *Market segmentation* is the process of dividing the overall market into groups of customers with similar characteristics. The objective is to select segments that match your strengths and are large enough to support your business. This does not mean you ignore the other market segments. It simply means that a high proportion of your sales will come from the market segment(s) you target. One of the strengths of being small is the ability to play 'nichemanship' in ways that large competitors cannot match.

Suppose you want to manufacture and sell packaged meals, and you are looking for a niche in this market. You could begin by segmenting households according to the dominant ways in which their meals are chosen, prepared, and consumed.

- *Country cooks* prepare three meals from scratch every day and occasionally make dessert. This market segment is not interested in packaged meals.
- *Functional feeders* look first for convenience, and then for variety and taste.
- *International eaters* are looking for exotic ways to enjoy ethnic foods.
- *Healthy households* are looking for natural foods and a balanced diet.
- *Grab-its* are typically the fast food, frozen dinner, takeaway eater.

Each segment represents a different group of customers with different buying motives. The objective is to target the segment that best matches your strengths. Your marketing strategy will emerge out of a clearly defined market niche, a thorough understanding of your customers' buying motives, and knowing exactly how your product or service is going to provide the benefits they want.

Positioning a business

The perfect market position is one that clearly establishes you as the preferred choice in your market niche. When you choose a market position for your business, make sure it accurately reflects the buying motives of your target market. The following buying motives are important to retail customers in forming an image of a business and what it offers.

Price	Quality
Assortment	Fashion
Personal selling	Convenience
Parking	Service
Display	Advertising
Atmosphere	Location

Your image depends on the relative value customers place on each buying motive. You can emphasise the ones that customers value most so that your market position exactly matches the benefits they want. You do this by developing value drivers that are aimed directly at satisfying customers' buying motives. Value drivers are the things your business does particularly well. Here are some examples.

Broader/deeper product lines	Loyal and well-trained staff
Lower costs and prices	Superior customer service
Unique products or services	More targeted marketing
Better quality or availability	More convenient location
Superior skills and experience	Serving a specialised market
A more pleasant atmosphere	Better parking

It only pays to develop value drivers that are effective in motivating customers to make a purchase. For example, you may have the most convenient location in town, but if customers' buying motive is lower prices, then they will probably drive long distances in order to save money. It is equally important that a value driver is something that can be advertised and promoted. For example, having lower prices is relatively easy to advertise and promote, but offering better service takes a little more explanation. Customers not only need to be aware of these value drivers, but they also need to be clear about how they satisfy their buying motives.

Products and services

The easiest and most profitable products and services to sell are the ones that your customers want to buy. The path to establishing a marketing strategy starts by identifying your customers' needs and then shaping your offering of products and services accordingly. A *product line* is a group of products or services that have similar characteristics and uses. For example, you would expect a computer store to offer product lines in desktops, laptops, tablets, printers, and software. The product lines that the computer store decides to carry are called its *product mix*. The key to deciding on the best product mix is how well it meets customers' needs.

The number of product lines on offer is called *product breadth*. If a computer store carries only laptops, then its product mix is narrow. If it carries every possible computer-related product line, then its product mix is wide. The assortment within a product line is called *product depth*. For example, the more models of laptops that a computer shop has for sale, the more depth it has in that product line. *Image anchors* are products that are heavily promoted because they define the image of the whole product line. They are usually from the higher end of the product line range. Decisions about product lines, product mix, product breadth, and product depth constitute your product and service strategy. It should be consistent with the way you have segmented the market and positioned your business.

Promotion

Promotion is the means by which you inform, persuade, and remind customers about the products and services you offer. Getting the word out is important because customers cannot buy what they don't know about. How you promote is built on a thorough understanding of your customers' buying motives and the way you position your business.

If you have spent considerable effort creating an image, then it is important to keep this in mind when selecting products and services for promotion. Deciding what to promote means focusing on customers' buying motives and developing a promotional theme around them. Here are some examples.

- Safety – people want to protect themselves and their property from harm.
- Savings – people are interested not only in the lowest price but also in savings through less frequent replacement, lower maintenance, or lower operating costs.
- Health – people buy products and services like exercise bikes, organic food, sunglasses, and aerobics classes to protect and maintain their health.
- Status – people buy things in order to be recognised. A fashion-conscious individual, for example, may be more concerned with the designer's name on the label than with the garment itself.
- Pleasure – people download movies, go to football games, and eat out at restaurants for pleasure.
- Convenience – many products and services make the routine chores of life easier. Examples are take-away food, house cleaning services, and car washes.

Your market area and your advertising budget will determine what medium, or combination of media, to use. There are traditional marketing media such as newspapers, magazines, direct mail, handbills, outdoor signs, radio, and television. Digital marketing media have become increasingly important in promoting an enormous variety of goods and services. These include email, social media platforms, having your own website, online advertising, and marketing on mobile devices. The time may be approaching when not being online will be perceived as odd and raise doubts about the business itself.

Deciding how much to spend on advertising and promotion is not only an important part of your marketing strategy, but it is also a key element in the cost side of your business. What sort of promotional effort is needed to achieve your sales goals, and what will it cost? Here are some factors that you may want to consider.

- Age – a new business needs more promotion than an established business.
- Products – a furniture store needs more promotion to attract customers than a pastry shop that relies on passing foot traffic.
- Location – a city bookstore needs more promotion to attract customers than an airport bookstore that relies on a captive market.
- Trading area – a farm equipment dealer serves a wider area and needs wider promotion than a city sandwich shop that serves a few nearby office buildings.
- Competition – more promotion may be needed in some situations to cope with competitive pressure.

Pricing

Too many small business operators undervalue their products and services. Profit is the reason you are in business, and profit is what enables you to stay in business. The objective is to set your prices in order to maximise profits, not to maximise sales turnover. An understanding of your market combined with a knowledge of the approaches to pricing will help you decide which pricing practices are best for your business. Here are some examples.

- Full-cost pricing – in which the price for each product or service must cover all of its direct costs, its portion of the overhead costs such as rent and electricity, and a mark-up for profit.
- Flexible mark-up pricing – uses full costs to establish a 'floor' price to which flexible mark-ups are added. Not only can you adjust your mark-ups to reflect changes in demand or competition, but this approach also provides for variations in the mark-up that you put on different product lines.
- Gross margin pricing – the customary practice in retail firms is to determine price by calculating a mark-up on the wholesale cost. The amount of the mark-up is called the gross margin. You don't apply the same mark-up to all items, nor do you use the same mark-ups at all times. The aim is to match the mark-ups to consumer demand in an effort to maximise profits.
- Going-rate pricing – for some firms, pricing does not involve a reference to the underlying costs. While they don't ignore costs, they pay more attention to competition and to the prices people are willing to pay.

- Suggested pricing – some businesses prefer not to make their own pricing decisions. Particularly in retailing, there is a tendency to accept the prices suggested by manufacturers or wholesalers for their products. If you use suggested prices, then you are accepting the manufacturer's pricing strategy as your own.
- Promotional pricing – discounting a popular item to generate traffic is promotional pricing. You might also carry some items that are not profitable because they regularly bring customers into your business. However, items that you carry exclusively don't face price competition and can stand greater mark-ups.
- Skimming versus penetration pricing – a skimming price is a high price that lasts for a short time to take advantage of early demand for a new product or service. A penetration price is a low price that encourages customers to try a new product or service in an effort to turn them into repeat customers.

Pricing practices vary between industry sectors. Retailers rely mostly on suggested pricing or going-rate pricing, with flexible mark-up pricing or gross margin pricing on more competitive product lines. Service firms typically calculate prices based on the time to perform a service multiplied by an hourly labour rate plus the materials used. The hourly labour rate is calculated to cover full costs and return a profit. Manufacturers tend towards full-cost pricing on exclusive lines and flexible mark-up pricing on competitive lines. Whatever approach to pricing you decide to use, don't forget to add GST to your prices.

Distribution

If products and services are not available where and when customers want them, then the sale is lost. Your goal is to identify the best way to get your products and services to your customers. Depending on the nature of your business your distribution may be simple and direct or it may involve multiple steps.

Direct marketing means dealing with customers yourself. The main advantages are that you don't have to share your profits and that you have complete control over the marketing process. There are other reasons why you might want to sell direct. You may be the only one who can demonstrate your products, offer detailed information about your products, or provide the right kind of personal or professional service. The flip side is that a distributor may have more resources and better expertise to sell your products and do it at a lower cost.

Beyond direct marketing, distribution becomes more complex and can take place on several levels. A one-level strategy uses just one intermediary. For consumer goods, it is usually a retailer, and for industrial goods, it is usually a distributor or agent. In larger markets, a two-level strategy might be more appropriate in which a manufacturer sells their product to a wholesaler who in turn distributes it to retailers. Distribution choices are equally important when selling services. Hotels, for example, not only sell their rooms (a service) directly, but they also sell through distributors such as travel agents, tour operators, airlines, tourism offices, and online booking systems. Sometimes more than one distribution channel is used. For example, customers for food supplements can buy them through health food stores, chemists, grocery stores, direct mail, and the Internet.

The choice of distribution is a trade-off between the cost of using intermediaries to achieve wider distribution versus the greater control and higher margins of selling direct. It has significant implications for your profit margins, marketing budget, final retail pricing, and your selling practices. If you are starting out, try to avoid costly or complex channels of distribution in favour of more direct methods in which volume requirements are lower and promotion is less expensive.

Marketing mix

The objective of a marketing strategy is to create a coordinated marketing programme that generates profitable sales. The way in which you combine the components of your marketing mix depends on how you choose to position your business. Here is a retail example of how the components of the marketing mix can be combined depending upon the market position that is chosen.

Position	Products	Promotion	Pricing	Distribution
Exclusive	Monopoly	Services	Highest	Personal
Speciality	Narrow/deep	Quality	Higher	Distinctive
Standard	Conventional	Availability	Going rate	Central
Discount	Broad	Price	Lowest	Extensive

An exclusive market position is usually the sole outlet for a particular product or service. The location need not be highly visible, but inside the atmosphere is plush and personal. Advertising is low key, refined and never refers to prices. Customers expect many extra services, and they are willing to pay for them.

A speciality market position depends on a narrow and very deep product line. The location and premises are distinctively related to the nature of the product. Advertising is primarily based on quality. Customers expect the firm to be an expert in its line of business and to offer quality products and services for which they are prepared to pay higher than average prices.

A standard market position carries conventional product lines but not the depth of a speciality outlet. Regular advertising is based on product availability and sometimes on price. Fewer services are offered, and customers expect them to be priced separately. Pricing policy usually follows suppliers' recommended prices with some adjustments for competition.

In a discount market position, customers expect little or no services in return for the lowest possible prices. Large amounts of advertising emphasise low prices, broad product lines, and convenient hours.

A customer's decision to buy from you depends on the effectiveness of your marketing mix. Customers look for products or services that meet their needs, wants, and desires. They respond to effective promotional programmes that create awareness, provide information, persuade, and remind them about what you offer. They are attracted by a price that represents value when compared with possible alternatives. And they want your product or service to be available when and where they want to buy it.

Summary

A marketing strategy consists of understanding your customers' buying motives, dividing your market into segments with similar characteristics, selecting the best segment(s) to target, positioning your product or service in the mind of your target market, and delivering the benefits your customers want to buy. Your marketing mix consists of offering the products and services that meet the needs and wants of your customers, at a price they are willing to pay, and offered where and when they want to buy them. It also includes the promotional methods used to inform customers about the products and services you have on offer. The objective is to combine the elements of the marketing mix so they will attract customers like a magnet.

5 Traditional marketing

Generating sales is the most important function in business. Without sales and the revenue stream it produces, none of the other business functions really matter. The purpose of this chapter is to examine traditional marketing methods including brochures, direct mail, newsletters, publicity, sponsorship, various forms of paid advertising, and important skills in personal selling. It is up to you to decide which of these methods will do the best job of informing, persuading, and reminding customers about your business and what it offers. In the next chapter, we will turn our attention to digital marketing.

In-house communications

Brochures are an important tool for retail and service businesses and an economical means of small-volume advertising. Brochures are more readily controlled than other forms of promotion because they are distributed by you and are inexpensive to produce. Brochures can be circulated wherever they are expected to give the greatest return, such as inside the business, inserted into packages, or delivered into letterboxes.

Direct mail has many of the advantages of a brochure, and it is also more dignified and personal because it can be directed to an individual customer. Direct mail is more selective than newspaper, radio, television, or brochures. To ensure controlled coverage, use a mailing list compiled from your own records or from commercially available mailing lists. Direct mail is more expensive than brochure advertising, but you can say more, you can try novel ideas on selected customers, and you can have a more personal touch.

A newsletter can be a potent promotional tool. Properly executed, it is an effective way to strengthen awareness and keep customers informed about your products and services. You can have a newsletter written and produced by a professional, or you can do it yourself using desktop publishing software on your personal computer. Most newsletters today are distributed by email because it eliminates most of the costs of a traditional newsletter.

Once you have established the purpose of your newsletter and defined its audience, there are a few things to think about. Newsletter information should reinforce your image. Topics commonly found in newsletters include a message

DOI: 10.4324/9781003394808-9

from the owner, news about the business, calendar of events, and articles about products and services. It should be information that is important to the reader. Publish your newsletter on a regular basis such as monthly, bimonthly, or quarterly. Keep in mind that it takes time and effort to prepare a newsletter, so the more frequently you decide to publish it, the more time you will need to devote to it. Your image is the key element in choosing a design. Once you have a design for the newsletter, keep it consistent from issue to issue. Photography keeps a newsletter from looking dull and too dense. Use only professional photos that are appealing and interesting.

Publicity

Publicity is an important supplement to advertising. There are all sorts of important events that can be used to generate publicity such as opening new premises, expansion, new products, and services, changes in opening hours and community projects. You can tell these stories with paid advertising, but publicity gets your story before the public for free. The newspaper will publish your story if it is news. What you do makes better news than what you say. It is up to you to write a press release. Lots of badly written press releases end up in the editor's rubbish bin. The best way to learn about writing press releases is to study the publicity that appears in your newspaper every day. Here are some tips.

- Use the word processing software on your personal computer to produce eye-catching press releases.
- Use simple words, short sentences, and try to avoid jargon and technical terminology. Give your press release a headline.
- Keep the press release to about 300 words, or about one page, and talk about your most important items first. Include a picture if it helps to tell the story.
- Email your press release so the newspaper can simply cut and paste.
- Remember to cover who, what, when, where, and why. Look for the unique, rare, or individual ingredient that makes your story newsworthy.
- Issue a press release before and after an event, but keep in mind that Mondays are not a good day for press releases.
- Be sure your name, telephone number, email address, and Internet address are clearly printed at the top of the press release.

Sponsorship

Sponsorship consists of underwriting an event like a fund-raiser or a local festival. Sponsorship support can be in the form of money, in-kind services, or products. Event sponsorship can yield a number of marketing opportunities, especially if you work closely with the event organiser to make sure you receive appropriate credit in publicity releases, brochures, advertising, programme books, street banners, and posters. The key to choosing the right sponsorship is to match the event with the nature of your business. Here are some things to consider.

- Demographics – what do you know about the event's audience, and do they represent your target market?
- Exclusivity – will there be many sponsors, or will your business stand out clearly as the sponsor of the event?
- Credits – what kind of exposure will you receive in terms of signs, event advertising, promotions, and public relations? For example, as a naming rights sponsor your business name should appear on all event materials.
- Credibility – does the event manager have a good track record for creating and managing successful events that produce a positive response from participants?
- Organisation – are there enough staff, volunteers, and resources to run the event?
- Timing – is it the right time to sponsor this event? Will it be popular?

Traditional advertising

The best way to advertise depends on your target market. Traditional advertising media consists of the local Yellow Pages, newspapers, radio stations, and television stations. You are looking for the best way to reach your target market in a format that enables you to tell your story that is cost-competitive with other choices.

Yellow pages

When people turn to the Yellow Pages, either the print version or the online version at **yellowpages.com.au**, they are usually ready to buy and looking for a supplier. They don't have to be persuaded to buy; they merely have to be persuaded to buy from you. Many businesses derive a significant proportion of their sales from Yellow Pages' advertising. One technique is to list everything you sell or do. For example, an insurance broker listed every type of insurance they sold. When customers look in the Yellow Pages, they are much more likely to read the entire advertisement so you can put more into it. If you have a website, feature your Internet address with the message that readers will find more information there.

Newspaper

For decades, newspapers were the primary advertising medium for small businesses. However, that has changed because many businesses have switched to buying online advertising where the ads are less expensive and they can reach a larger market. This raises the question, is it worth it to advertise in the newspaper? The answer is 'yes' if you are selling consumer goods and services in a local area and you advertise in a local newspaper. Local newspapers are typically community or suburban papers that publish community news and events. For some local businesses or businesses that target older or less digitally engaged audiences, local newspaper advertising can still be a good choice. There are two types of newspaper advertising – classified ads and display ads.

Classified ads

An inexpensive classified ad in the local newspaper can deliver customers who are looking for a product or service. Moreover, if the ad appears regularly, it builds future business by establishing your name and building your image. Classified advertisements are typically very brief. There is a section of the newspaper set aside for 'classifieds' and they are grouped into various categories.

People typically read the classifieds to solve a problem. The most effective classified ads speak directly to solving a problem. The first couple of words should tell readers about the most important benefit your product or service offers. Keep it short and commanding by telling them what you sell, who should buy it, and how to find you. If your competitors have been using classified advertising, then it's likely to work for you too. Look for their keywords and use them in your own ads. Do they mention a benefit? How do they get the reader's attention? The way to tell which classified ads work best is to test different versions. Run each ad long enough to give it a fair go before deciding which one to run on a regular basis.

Display ads

Display ads are larger and more expensive than classified ads, and they appear alongside the newspaper's stories. They are graphically designed ads that may contain logos, photos, and borders in addition to text. Display advertising works well for businesses that fit into a specific section of the newspaper. For example, a travel agent can run ads in the travel section of the paper. Pursued with taste, vigour, and imagination, display advertising in a local newspaper can attract new customers, retain existing customers, and help establish your image.

Magazines

General consumer magazines are not only an expensive advertising medium, but their coverage is far too wide for a local market. Special interest magazines are less costly, and you can reach people who are actively thinking about pursuing their particular interest. Examples include gardening, photography, skiing, golf, boating, cooking, weddings, parenting, and computers. Special interest magazines are especially useful for mail-order businesses that target a national market with a narrow product line.

Radio

Radio advertising is almost entirely local advertising. Some products can be advertised better by voice than in print. Other products benefit from radio advertising as a complement to print advertising. The human voice can establish rapport with listeners. The human voice can also convey a sense of urgency. Customers must be listening to the radio for your message to get through. That is why choice of station, choice of broadcast times, and repetition are important. Use a station that has strong listener appeal for your type of customer. Each station defines its listening audience by age, musical taste, interest, and geographical market. If your target market is baby boomers, then you would select a station that plays their music. Try to get time slots when your customers listen to the radio. For example, commercials for a plant nursery will reach more prospects if they run during a gardening programme. The non-visual message is short-lived, and many radio listeners are 'tuned out' or concentrating on something else while they listen. That is why the key is to repeat your message frequently.

Television

Sight, sound, colour, and motion make this medium the closest thing to personal selling, and it takes place right in the customer's own home. Like radio, you need to be very careful to select the station and the broadcast times that match your target audience. Television is a medium that can carry action, so you should capitalise on it. For example, a boat dealer should feature a boat slicing through the water as opposed to a still picture. Television advertising can be expensive, especially when you factor in the cost of production. The cost also depends on the length of the ad, the time slot, and how often it is played.

Repetition in television advertising is different from radio. It is boring to see the same television commercial repeated too often. Think in terms of short, interchangeable segments that can be mixed and matched to make your television commercials appear different. The beginning and end of every commercial should consistently identify your business and its image, but the message in the middle can change for variety and interest.

Outdoor advertising

Outdoor advertising includes billboards, posters, transit advertising such as buses, railways, trams, and taxis, and others such as bus and train shelters, kiosks, phone booths, and seating. Vehicle signage is popular amongst retail and service businesses. Couriers, removalists, and home service operators with distinctive vehicle signage are advertising their services while they are working. Visit the Outdoor Media Association website at *oma.org.au* for ideas about how you might use outdoor advertising.

Personal selling

What is it about personal selling that worries so many small business operators? Some avoid it because they have a fear of rejection. Others dislike selling because they think it consists of tricking or coercing a customer to buy something they don't really need. Personal selling is an essential part of being in business, and it can be done in a way that is positive, rewarding, and enjoyable. If the product or service offered truly meets the customer's needs, then everyone benefits as a result of the sale. It means taking the time to build a relationship with your customer rather than just focusing on making an immediate sale. Although it may take a little longer to produce the first sale, you will be rewarded long into the future with repeat business and referrals from satisfied customers.

Customers want to be served by someone they can trust. Do you find yourself going back again and again to someone who is helpful and honest? Something extraordinary happens when you give a customer your undivided attention. It means listening and not interrupting them or impatiently waiting to talk next. When you listen more than you talk, customers realise you are interested in them. Personal selling is a way of doing business that is flexible, cooperative, and professional. The following steps are a guide.

- Know your product or service – before you begin a conversation with a customer, it is important that you clearly understand your products and services and why people should want to buy them.
- Make the initial contact – a courteous greeting establishes rapport between you and your customer. The traditional 'May I help you?' often results in an answer like 'Just looking' which fails to get the ball rolling. Simply, 'Good morning, what can I do for you today?' is a more positive greeting.
- Exchange information – this step consists of asking questions, uncovering buying motives, giving information, and determining how your product or service will fulfil the customer's needs. Find out why the customer has an interest in buying a particular product or service. The most effective questions are those that are not answered with a simple 'yes' or 'no'. Instead, try using open-ended questions that get the customer talking. These are questions that begin with words like 'Why', 'What', or 'How'.
- Propose a solution – once you are comfortable with the relationship you have created, propose how your product or service will solve the customer's problem or fulfil their need by focusing on the link between its features and benefits. A feature is a distinctive characteristic of a product or service. A benefit is the way the customer's buying motive is fulfilled by the feature.
- Confirm the sale – rather than focusing on 'closing the sale', a term that indicates the end of the process, confirming the sale means you are reviewing the customer's willingness and ability to make a commitment. It is a natural extension of a relationship built on a foundation of trust, respect, and rapport.

- Deliver the goods – actually delivering the product or service is a very important step. First, if you don't deliver, then you haven't completed the sale. Second, during this step, you have an excellent opportunity to continue to build trust and to cement your relationship with the customer.
- Follow up promptly – find out how the customer likes your product or service. This provides you with an opportunity to create repeat business and to ask for referrals to new customers. If there is a problem, then you are there to correct it. And don't forget to thank them for their patronage.

The main reason so many individuals shy away from selling is because they don't like to be turned down. This is a basic and understandable human reaction. A customer will generally say 'no' because they genuinely don't want to buy what you are offering. If you focus on building a sincere relationship, then they may return to make a purchase later or refer others who are interested.

Summary

Generating sales revenue is the most important function in business, and there are a variety of traditional marketing tools including brochures and direct mail, newsletters, publicity, and sponsorship. When it comes to paid advertising, you want media that reach your target market, enable you to tell your story effectively, and are within your advertising budget. The main choices are the Yellow Pages, classified and display newspaper advertising, magazine advertising, radio and television advertising, and outdoor advertising. Small businesses have the advantage of being in close personal contact with their customers, and personal selling is an important part of traditional marketing methods. It is up to you to decide which of these methods will do the best job of informing, persuading, and reminding customers about your business and what you offer.

6   Digital marketing

The term *digital marketing* includes email marketing tools, social media networks, online marketplaces, online directories, websites, blogs, search engines, mobile devices, and more. While traditional marketing methods are effective media for many small businesses, they have limitations when it comes to how many people they can reach, how well they can engage with them, and how accurately their effectiveness can be measured. Ultimately, both traditional and digital marketing methods are aimed at connecting with customers in the right place, at the right time, with the right message.

Some digital marketing methods deliver better results than traditional marketing methods because you can target audiences that range from purely local to international. You also have the ability to target specific age groups, geographic locations, occupations, interests, and more. Thanks to a variety of online tools, you can check on your results, focus on what is working, and revise what is not. One of the most crucial advantages of digital marketing is that it enables you to build a personal relationship with each customer by making it possible for them to research your products and services, 'like' and 'follow' your business, rate their experiences with your business and its offerings, and share this information with other prospective customers. The purpose of this chapter is to examine how digital marketing can be used in a small business.

Importance of digital marketing

Digital marketing has important consequences for every marketing strategy because it represents powerful new marketing channels. *Brick-and-click* digital marketing is used by traditional businesses that want to take advantage of the Internet as part of their overall marketing mix. *Pure-click* digital marketing is conducted wholly in cyberspace without any need for a physical place of business. Email is a digital marketing tool that can be targeted at specific customers, while social media can be used to target like-minded groups. A website is not only a versatile advertising medium, but it can also take orders and payments. Mobile technology is the most recent addition to the digital marketing arsenal.

DOI: 10.4324/9781003394808-10

A retail business that is marketing online is called an *e-tailer*. A pure-click e-tailer only operates through their website. A catalogue e-tailer operates a traditional mail order business with a web-based catalogue. A brick-and-click e-tailer operates a traditional retail establishment augmented by a website. A manufacturing business that sells its products directly to customers online can shorten its distribution channel and capture greater retail margins.

Digital marketing is effective in bringing buyers and sellers together. Some web sites act as a virtual broker with a full range of services including listing, negotiation, transaction, payment, and delivery. Some websites conduct auctions for sellers, while others search out hard-to-find goods and services for buyers. There are also websites that facilitate transactions between buyers and sellers by providing comparison shopping information and services without actually engaging in the exchange of money or goods. High-volume websites such as Yahoo!, Amazon, and eBay offer hosting services for online retailers known as virtual shopping malls or online marketplaces.

Digital marketing has also spawned new types of businesses. For example, some deal in virtual products such as music downloads or smartphone apps. Others create content that attracts targeted users who *click-through* to other businesses that pay for the click-throughs. Some charge a subscription fee for access to text, audio, or video content. A powerful new force in digital marketing is social media, in which users have the means to connect with other like-minded individuals. The resulting high-volume traffic provides enormous opportunities for targeted advertising, subscription services, and premium content.

Email marketing

Email marketing is an efficient way to stay connected with your customers and promote your business without needing to pay for lots of print space, radio or television time, or the associated production costs. Email advertising is also quite a bargain compared with the cost of direct mail, and the response rates are typically much higher. Links in emails can be used to guide customers to your website. Email marketing tools enable you to monitor who opens your email and who clicks on a link. The main challenge of email marketing is building your list of contacts. You can invite people to join your email list on your website, you can encourage referrals, and you can buy email databases of people who have agreed to receive emails.

A common email advertising tool is a newsletter. Ask customers to sign up for your email newsletter by advertising benefits such as informative content or early notification of special offers. Email newsletters are read far more carefully when they offer information that is genuinely useful rather than merely selling products or services. Helpful tips, engaging content, and humour are important qualities in email newsletters. There are a number of commercial services available that can help you manage bulk emails and email marketing campaigns.

These services provide tools to help you create emails, send them out at nominated times to your email list, personalise the address field, and report on how many were read.

Social media marketing

Social media is not to everyone's taste, but for some businesses, it can be a powerful online marketing tool to increase sales and create deeper customer relationships. The range of social media includes blogs, forums, social networking platforms, and content-hosting websites. They are used for customer ratings and reviews, user recommendations and referrals, or sharing the experience of shopping online. One of the great benefits of social media is the ability to read reviews about a product or service. Peer recommendations play a key role when online shoppers are getting ready to make a purchase.

There are two ways to integrate social media into your digital marketing strategy. You can host social media tools as part of your website, or you can provide links to established social media platforms. Social media platforms offer a variety of features. Your *profile* is the front page for your business. *Like* or *Thumbs Up* indicates the viewer found your content interesting and has *engaged* with it. These are usually good indicators that your content is working, so you can confidently post more in this style. A *Follower* or *Fan* is someone who is interested in your page. The number of followers you have is important, but it is the rate of engagement that matters most. Every social media user has a *feed* in which content from a variety of sources appears including other social media users and your profile and posts. You can add *hashtags* to your content that consist of the hashtag character (#) followed by a word that describes that content. Hashtags act like a search function, enabling you to add your content to other content that shares the same hashtag. This means your content will reach a wider audience because it is more likely to show up in searches that use the hashtag terms.

There is a risk with social media because you cannot control what people may say about your business, your products, or your services. If their comments are complimentary and they recommend you to others it will trigger a viral response that is better than any advertising you can buy. If you attract criticism, however, then the damage can be enormous. It is usually better to learn from negative feedback rather than to ignore it. By monitoring compliments and criticisms, you can learn much about how to improve your business and your image.

Types of platforms

Blogs are platforms on which users can have an informal conversation about a particular topic. The blog owner usually writes an opinion piece and invites readers to respond with their comments. A conversation is known as a *thread*. You can create a blog on your own website or participate in blogs that are related to your line of business. *Forums* are more formal online discussion sites in which the messages are usually moderated before they are posted.

Social networks are all-purpose social media platforms in which people interact and share information and experiences. Facebook, Twitter, and LinkedIn are examples of popular social network platforms. Social networking platforms also enable customers to share their purchasing experience and to make and receive personal recommendations. On some platforms, customers can bring products or services to the attention of their online friends and followers using a *share* or *like* button.

Content-hosting websites make it possible to upload photos, audio, or video content to provide a more engaging presentation of products and services. *Podcasts* are downloadable audio files that provide sound such as a talk or a lecture. *Photo sharing* applications, such as Pinterest, can be used to present still pictures. *Video sharing* sites, such as YouTube, are used to present video content.

Popular platforms

Facebook at *facebook.com* commands the biggest audience. The 18–39 age group is the most active, but the 65+ age group is the fastest growing. Females tend to be slightly more active than males. It enables users to post information and updates, distribute a variety of multimedia content, and communicate with customers and the public. Ad creation tools are simple due to a well-designed interface. Campaigns range from those designed to attract more *likes* to those designed to drive traffic to your website. Facebook *Messenger* is integrated with your page, so you can connect with individual customers to answer questions and receive feedback. Using Facebook's audience targeting tools, you can selectively advertise to the demographics that make sense for your business, and you can keep an eye on the results.

Pinterest at *pinterest.com.au* is a visual bookmarking tool that helps users post, discover, and save creative ideas. You will need to sign up for a *Pinterest for Business* account to access all of the business tools. Visitors consist mainly of younger women, but recent growth has seen increasing numbers of older women as well. Users can surf the Pinterest platform and 'pin' (bookmark) content that interests them. When your business is linked to Pinterest, users can easily navigate back to your website by selecting the pin bookmark. Those who have been 'pinning' for a while create a snapshot of who they are and what they find interesting. This enables you to target your marketing based on their pin profiles. Food, crafts, and beauty products typically do well on Pinterest.

Twitter at *twitter.com* is a close competitor to Facebook in terms of audience size, but the advertising options are more limited. It is a platform on which you can broadcast short messages, called *tweets*, that are limited in length. Twitter users who follow you will find your tweets in a list called their *Twitter stream*. Compelling content will help you attract new followers and keep them engaged. Twitter is popular with social media users under the age of 50 who use it because they are looking for real-time updates from sources they consider to be reliable. Use your business name as your Twitter name and use your logo as your Twitter picture. You can post brief messages, photos, and videos, link to additional content, and communicate with customers and the public. The *Promoted Tweet* option puts your tweets at the top of a selected number of users' news feeds. You can identify your core demographics, but the criteria you can choose from are more restricted than on Facebook.

LinkedIn at *au.linkedin.com* is a powerful marketing tool if you sell primarily to other businesses. It also appeals to professionals more than Facebook or Twitter. It is particularly useful if you are targeting a specific type of professional. You will need to build a LinkedIn business page in order to get access to all of the features. The *Sponsored Updates* option is good for increased visibility. It has an easy interface that enables you to set it up in a few minutes. You can get assistance with targeting your audience.

YouTube at *youtube.com* is owned by Google and offers a number of advertising options including video ads and static advertising associated with videos. It does not offer much control over your target audience, and ads are a little more expensive than on some other social platforms. However, it has been shown to be effective in raising brand awareness and driving purchasing decisions. Common video themes that are used by businesses include tutorials showing how to use a product, testimonials with a satisfied customer, and behind-the-scenes videos such as a tour of a business.

Instagram at *instagram.com* is a photo-sharing, video-sharing, and social networking service owned by Facebook that enables you to take pictures and videos and share them either publicly or privately. Although it can be viewed on a desktop computer, Instagram is primarily a mobile app. There are three different formats for advertising. *Photo Ads* look like regular photo posts, but they have a 'Sponsored' label above the photo and a 'Learn More' button under the photo. *Video Ads* are regular video posts with a Sponsored label on top. *Carousel Ads* look identical to photo ads but feature multiple photos that users can swipe.

Marketplaces and directories

Amazon at *amazon.com.au* is a marketplace that provides access to a massive audience. It provides you with the capability to sell your products directly on Amazon or reach Amazon customers through Amazon website display advertisements. You can provide essential information about your products and services, availability, prices, hours of operation, contact information, and delivery. It also enables you to read and respond to reviews posted by customers.

Etsy at *etsy.com/au* is also a marketplace where people connect to buy and sell goods. Producers use Etsy to sell what they make or create. Shoppers use Etsy to look for things they want to buy. Some manufacturers partner with Etsy sellers to promote sales of their products.

eBay at *ebay.com.au* is another marketplace for buyers and sellers to come together to buy and sell almost anything. A seller lists an item and either accepts auction bids for it or sets a fixed price. For *Buy It Now* listings, the first buyer to pay the fixed price gets the item. For online auction listings, a buyer either buys the item outright for a fixed price or places a bid on it. The bidding remains open for a certain number of days, and the buyer with the highest bid can make the purchase.

Yelp at *business.yelp.com.au* is an online directory and a social media network. It provides a free suite of tools to showcase your business. You can create a free Yelp Business Page to upload photos, add a link to your website, and maintain your contact information. You can also establish a Business Owner Account to respond to customer reviews, and you can promote your business through Yelp Ads.

TripAdvisor at *tripadvisor.com.au* is also an online directory and a social media network. It is the world's largest travel site, enabling travellers to plan and book trips. It also offers reviews from millions of travellers. TripAdvisor is *open sourced*, which means that once you create an account, you have little or no control over what is posted in reviews. TripAdvisor reviews are particularly important for businesses in tourism and hospitality.

Your own website

A website can be designed to achieve different objectives. Some businesses have a website that is simply an online brochure that complements their overall advertising programme. Other businesses have a website that goes one step further by offering customer service, product specifications, or answers to customer inquiries. Businesses that sell consumer products typically go beyond advertising and customer support to include online ordering and credit card approval. According to the Australian Bureau of Statistics, about 40 per cent of small businesses have a website, and more than half of them use it to generate orders. Before you contemplate launching a website, look at some examples of other commercial websites. Pay particular attention to websites for businesses like your own. Look for common elements and evaluate how they might work for you.

- Content – what does the website have to offer? Does it provide useful information about products and services? Does it help you understand the nature of the business? Is valuable information provided that you cannot get elsewhere? Is it updated regularly?
- Image – is the use of graphics, colour, and logos consistent throughout the website? Can you tell just by looking at each page that this website belongs to this particular business? Does the website establish and reaffirm the market position of the business?
- Ease of navigation – is it simple to move around the site? Do you know where you are, where you have been, and where you can go next? Do you have to scroll up and down or back and forth to view parts of the page? Are the links effective? Can you find your way through the website without having to go back to the home page?

- Useability – does the website provide information that is helpful? Does it do a good job? Do you come away with the feeling that you would like to return to the site again?

The digital revolution has made it easier than ever to make a niche business sustainable. It has also become much easier to start a business in the first place because you can register a domain name and use an online website builder to get up and running within a day. If you are new to digital marketing, there are services that can design and install a website for you and show you how to use it. If you are on a budget, there are some simple and cost-effective techniques you can implement yourself. Most customers start their journey by searching on Google, Bing, or other search engines, so you need to create content for your website that answers their queries.

Keywords are words that describe your business. For example, if you are a plumber, keywords for your website might be 'plumber', 'blocked pipe', and 'dripping faucet'. The keywords are what a customer uses when they search Google or Bing looking for products and services. The search engine websites each have a section that helps you find the best keywords for your business. If you don't put the right keywords into your content, then no one will be able to find you on the search engines. A word of caution, however, if you use the same keywords too often, Google will register this as spam. Including a keyword three to five times seems to be optimal. Keep in mind that a website requires constant attention. Can you commit to adding new content regularly? Do you have the time and money to support it properly? If you're not willing to do this yourself, can you afford to hire someone to do it for you?

Online advertising

Online advertising is basically an extension of traditional advertising. Some websites provide targeted content mixed with advertising messages such as banner advertisements. Other websites are designed to be an online version of classified advertising. There are also websites that use video and audio segments like a television infomercial, and there are a few with interactive advertising that requires users to respond to the advertisement before reaching the content they are after.

Traditional advertising attempts to *push* a message out to the largest possible audience in the hope of catching the attention of a few potential customers. While push advertising will not disappear, the marketing landscape is changing. People have been bombarded with irrelevant advertising messages for too long, and they are turning to the Internet, where they can choose which websites to visit, what to click on, and what information they *pull* onto their screen. The Internet provides them with broad and deep access to detailed information about the products and services that really interest them.

Pay Per Click (PPC) advertising is a marketing method in which you pay a fee when your ad is clicked by a viewer, sending them to your website. Search engine advertising is one of the most popular forms of PPC. You bid for an ad placement in a search engine's sponsored links. When a viewer searches using a keyword that is related to your business, your ad appears. Google Ads at ***ads. google.com*** is a popular platform that enables users to create ads that appear on Google's search engine and other Google platforms.

Google My Business at ***google.com/intl/en_au/business/*** is a tool that enables you to list yourself as a local business. It includes information about your business, such as opening hours, website link, call and direction buttons, and enables you to receive and manage Google reviews. If your business relies on website traffic from local customers, then a Google My Business account should be registered, optimised, and regularly kept up to date.

Mobile marketing

Smartphones, tablets, and other mobile devices are so widespread that many businesses are using them to engage with their customers. Mobile marketing is similar to other digital channels, using text, graphics, and voice messages. SMS messaging is one form of mobile marketing that sends announcements to mobile phone users. It has been used in combination with other applications, such as location-based advertising, to deliver messages to mobile subscribers who come into range of an advertising business like a restaurant, cafe, or movie theatre. Search engine marketing is another mobile marketing channel in which customers can look for instant information while they are on the go.

Brick-and-click retailers can take advantage of mobile marketing using applications such as barcode scanning and push notifications to improve the customer's shopping experience. These enable customers to access the benefits of shopping online, such as product reviews, while shopping in-store. It bridges the gap between online shopping and in-store shopping, and it is a way for retailers to compete with the lower prices typically available online.

Using a mobile browser, which is a web browser on a mobile device, customers can shop online without having to be at their personal computer. Catalogue merchants can deliver their catalogue electronically and take orders from the customer's mobile device. Mobile marketers can also accept a variety of credit cards and other payment systems from mobile devices. Tickets can be booked and cancelled on a mobile device with the help of simple apps or by accessing the portals of various agents. Location-based services use the geographical position of the mobile device to identify the location of the nearest restaurant or taxi rank. Other examples of location-based services include entertainment or social events in a particular area, finding a business or service, navigation instructions to an address, and receiving alerts.

Summary

Digital marketing methods offer high-tech alternatives to traditional marketing including email marketing, social media marketing, online marketplaces, online directories, having your own website, online advertising, and mobile marketing. Digital marketing methods are capable of delivering valuable results because you are able to target audiences that range from purely local to international, and you can target particular age groups, geographic locations, occupations, customer interests, and more. A big advantage of digital marketing is that it enables you to build a close relationship with customers by assisting them to make enquiries about your products and services, encouraging feedback about their experiences with your business, and they can share this information with others who may be interested in becoming customers.

Part B

Reality check

Can the target market be captured?

The purpose of these questions is to help you decide if the target market for an idea can be captured. We are looking for evidence of good prospects for anticipated demand, market acceptance, and market strength. For each question, select the answer that best describes your idea. Your responses will help you form a judgement about whether or not you think the market for your idea can be captured. The responses will also become part of the Commercial Feasibility Rating in the Appendix.

Anticipated demand

Questions about demand are easier to ask than to answer because we need to know how the marketplace operates. There is always a certain amount of judgement involved about the factors that are important in influencing demand. Nevertheless, demand can be examined in the early stages by looking at the general behaviour of the marketplace and how related products and services are selling. An objective analysis of demand is crucial to assessing market viability. It is easy to overestimate market size and misjudge its growth and stability. These mistakes can be commercially critical, even for an exceptionally good idea. An evaluation of an idea's commercial lifespan and the potential for further spinoffs explores demand even further.

Market size

Evaluating the relative size of the market is an essential part of anticipating demand. What we are looking for is information about the overall size of the market, even though not every customer is going to buy from us. To make a reasonable approximation of market size, consider the characteristics of the idea and the market environment in which it is likely to be sold. The target market might be a neighbourhood or a suburb, a town or city, a region, a state, Australia-wide, or global. The number of customers can be in terms of individuals, households, businesses, or some other customer unit. What is the problem, want, or need that the idea will solve? Why is this problem important? Who will buy the product or service if this problem can be solved? How many potential customers are reachable and receptive in the target market area?

DOI: 10.4324/9781003394808-11

The larger the market, the more likely there will be significant demand. A limited market involves more risk than a larger one because small or local markets cannot sustain high development costs, making it more difficult to launch and exploit an idea. Similarly, high promotion, distribution, or service costs are not usually compatible with ideas of limited market size because higher costs and fewer potential customers make for limited prospects.

11. Will the size of the target market for my idea be . . .

    a)   very large – appealing to practically every individual?
    b)   large – appealing to at least one person in every household or business?
    c)   medium – appealing to a distinctive group of consumers or businesses?
    d)   small – appealing to a narrow group of consumers or businesses?
    e)   very small – appealing to a highly specialised or very limited group of consumers or businesses?

Market growth

Whereas market size refers to the current potential of the target market, market growth refers to how market size is expected to change over time. It is important to be clear about market growth because one of the biggest mistakes is forecasting unrealistic growth rates. Even if growth in market size is likely, it does not automatically follow that you will capture it.

Will the market increase, remain constant, or decline? An expanding market clearly implies more opportunities and the possibility of greater financial returns. A declining market usually means the opposite. At first glance, a constant market size might appear to be predictable and therefore of low or modest risk. However, if competitors are a serious threat, a new player might struggle to capture market share unless the idea has significant competitive strength. To reach its potential, an idea that enjoys a large and rapidly expanding market needs to be in the hands of someone who has the expertise and the resources to fully exploit it.

Trying to estimate market growth faces the same obstacles as trying to estimate market size. For existing products and services, there is usually information about past sales and the rate of growth. For new products and services or new market ideas, estimating market growth is more complicated. Sometimes estimates can be inferred from the growth rates of comparable products or comparable markets. For these, an estimate of the initial market size is the critical question. Estimating the growth rate is of less importance because no one really knows anything about growth rates until the idea is tested.

12. Will the rate of growth in the target market for my idea be likely to . . .

    a)   increase rapidly?
    b)   increase gradually?
    c)   be constant?

d) decline gradually?
e) decline rapidly?

Market stability

Whereas market size refers to the current market and market growth refers to the likely future change in market size, market stability refers to the pattern of demand. Almost all products and services face fluctuations in demand. For some, variations in demand can be foreseen with reasonable accuracy, permitting forward planning for inventory and staff to cover surges and lulls. Beauty salons experience increased demand on Fridays and Saturday mornings. A sandwich shop in the office district will have increased demand at lunch times on weekdays, while an intimate restaurant will experience more demand in the evening on Fridays and Saturdays. Cinemas have more patrons on the weekends and on nearly all holidays. Health clubs experience demand peaks in the early morning and in the evening when most members are not working.

Unstable demand that does not behave according to any well-defined seasonal or cyclical pattern is a more hazardous proposition. Sometimes it is affected by unpredictable events such as a strike, drought, fad, the threat of war, or other random disturbance. Variations sometimes occur for no apparent reason when customers suddenly and simultaneously converge on a particular business. At other times, they are mysteriously absent. The important point is that some ideas are more susceptible to erratic demand instability than others.

13. Will fluctuations in demand for my idea be . . .

a) highly stable – not susceptible to fluctuations?
b) stable – modest variations that can be accurately foreseen?
c) predictable – variations that can be reasonably foreseen?
d) unstable – susceptible to moderately unpredictable fluctuations?
e) highly unstable – subject to severely unpredictable fluctuations?

Commercial lifespan

Some ideas have a short commercial life, whereas others enjoy a long one. An idea might last only a few months, like a fashion accessory, compared with more than a century for the motor car. Commercial lifespan can apply to a product, a process, a service, a business, a brand, a style, a fashion, or a fad. It characterises how an idea moves from inspiration to exhaustion over its commercial life.

The first stage in the commercial lifespan of a new idea is the introduction stage. The main goal is to establish a market and build demand. High costs combined with low sales volume typically produce a period of losses, and the risk of failure is high. If an idea survives the introduction stage, it generally enters the growth stage, in which the main goals are gaining customer preference and increasing sales. The growth stage is a welcome relief from the introduction stage, but it is also a period of hard work, continuing stress, low returns, and high risk. If an idea safely navigates the growth stage, it is ready to enter the harvest stage, in which efficiency is at its peak, costs are under control, and profit margins are at their best. Ideas for which a long harvest stage is expected are a safer basis on which to launch a business. It does not make sense to make a long-term financial commitment or invest in specialised assets for ideas with a limited commercial lifespan.

14. Will the harvest stage for my idea be likely to last for a . . .

    a)   very long time?
    b)   reasonably long time?
    c)   moderate period of time?
    d)   somewhat limited time?
    e)   very brief time?

Spinoffs

Spinoffs are additional products or services that can be derived from the original idea. If an idea can be extended to other products or services, then it has greater commercial potential. For example, Coca-Cola has varied its traditional formula to offer Cherry Coke, Vanilla Coke, Caffeine Free Coke, Diet Coke, and Coke Zero. An example of spinoffs in a service business is a childcare centre that expanded their business by offering family counselling and parenting courses. There were few extra costs, and the new services fit perfectly with the existing business. More than half of the new products and services introduced each year are spinoffs of other products or services. The benefits that come from spinoffs include more customers, more sales to existing customers, greater marketing efficiency, lower costs, and greater profits.

15. Will the potential for additional related products or services be . . .

    a)   very high – many spinoffs are likely?
    b)   high – a few spinoffs are likely?
    c)   moderate – a few spinoffs are possible?
    d)   limited – minor variations only?
    e)   very limited – this is a one-off product or service only?

Market acceptance

In the last section, we were concerned with establishing the anticipated demand for a new idea. In this section, we go a step further by exploring if customers are likely to accept the idea. The two sections are analogous to estimating how many trout there are in a stream and how well your bait will attract them. If they like the bait, then you will catch fish. But if they don't like the bait, then it does not matter how many trout there are in the stream.

This section explores five important questions that affect how the market may react to a new idea. Does it fulfil a genuine need? Will the benefits be easy to recognise? Is it compatible with existing attitudes and patterns of use? Is it complicated to consume or use? Will it be difficult and/or costly to distribute?

An example of market acceptance can be found in the history of photography. The introduction of the Brownie camera by Kodak founder George Eastman in 1900 transformed photography from a technically challenging, costly, professional activity to a simple mass market product. He did not seek market acceptance based on the sophistication of his new technology. Instead, he showed people how simple and fun it was to take pictures. Later on, instant photography was introduced, offering a new benefit of on-the-spot images. Today, digital photography has replaced instant photography because it is not only less expensive, but it also satisfies the evolving needs of computer savvy customers. The key to commercial success over a century of modern photography has been market acceptance. Every time the technology evolved, the market got a better solution that was easy to understand, compatible with their expectations, simple to use, and easy to buy.

Need

The success of an idea depends on its ability to fulfil a genuine need. A need can take different forms such as functional needs, psychological needs, economic needs, social needs, or informational needs. The most basic needs include things like safety, savings, health, status, pleasure, and convenience. Needs have different degrees of importance, ranging from essential to non-essential. Successful businesses have an intimate understanding of what these needs are and how they can meet them. Ensuring that an idea meets a genuine need means doing some homework to find out what features and benefits customers really want to buy.

Customers with the same basic needs can have different wants. Although basic needs are relatively broad, customer wants are usually quite narrow. A want is a desire for a specific product or service to satisfy the underlying need. For example, you need to eat when you are hungry. What you want to eat depends on things like the time of day, the food you like, and what is available.

The best ideas fulfil an essential need that is highly valued. Other ideas may fulfil a need, but not necessarily one that is highly valued. And some ideas are simply novelties that are easily forgotten. Creating a product or service that offers real benefits and tangible value means ensuring it is fully aligned with the needs and wants of the customer. A want does not become a sale, however, unless the customer also has the ability and willingness to pay for it.

16. Will the need fulfilled by my idea be . . .

    a)   very high – an essential need that is highly valued?

    b)   high – a nonessential need that is nevertheless highly valued?

c) moderate – an essential need of average value?
d) low – a nonessential need of average value?
e) very low – a superficial need that is relatively unimportant?

Recognition

Customers must be able to recognise the features and benefits of an idea before it can gain their acceptance. The cost and effort required to explain the features and benefits varies substantially from one idea to another. Will customers find an idea easy to understand? Can they try it out before committing themselves? Can they observe its performance before they buy it? Can it be favourably compared with something in which they have previously had some experience? Genuine need, compatibility, and simplicity are among the elements that drive recognition. We are constantly bombarded with information about new products and services. We cope with this by shutting out those things that are inconsistent with our prior knowledge and experience. That is why recognition depends so much on how well an idea aligns with customers' existing attitudes and beliefs.

17. Will the features and benefits of my idea be . . .

a) very obvious – completely self-evident?
b) obvious – easy to understand?
c) noticeable – but requiring some explanation?
d) obscure – not apparent and requiring substantial explanation?
e) very obscure – not apparent and difficult and/or costly to explain?

Compatibility

People can reject a new idea for any number of irrational reasons such as 'I can't be bothered' or 'I'm fine the way I am.' They are generally comfortable with existing products or services because that is what they already know and understand. Once formed, these attitudes and beliefs are difficult to change. For example, an idea for an instant version of a popular food could turn out to be incompatible with customers' perceptions if they think it is going to taste different.

Compatibility is the way in which an idea is consistent with customers' existing values, past experiences, and perceived needs. Innovation is the way in which an idea diverges from a previous solution and offers a better one. Even though an innovation may represent an improvement, it can put an idea outside the normal expectations of potential buyers. The trade-off is between ideas that represent incremental change thereby maximising compatibility, and ideas for radical change that offer the benefits of innovation. If the expectations, attitudes. and beliefs of potential customers are entrenched, then it is important to protect compatibility in order to achieve market acceptance.

18. Will the compatibility of my idea with established customer behaviour be . . .

    a)   very high – completely consistent with customer behaviour?
    b)   high – reasonably consistent with customer behaviour?
    c)   moderate – might be a slight conflict with customer behaviour?
    d)   low – considerable conflict with customer behaviour?
    e)   very low – extreme conflict with customer behaviour?

Complexity

Complexity refers to how difficult a product or service will be to use or consume. The amount of learning needed to overcome complexity directly affects market acceptance because it introduces an element of risk in the customer's mind. This is especially true of new technological ideas. The technological sophistication of these products is often ahead of the people who are meant to use them. They fear technology because they cannot understand it. The more complicated the idea, the more customers have to learn. The more customers have to learn, the more difficult it is to gain their acceptance.

Complexity is also a barrier to market acceptance if the process of making a purchase decision is challenging. Some purchase decisions are more difficult than others and require more effort. For example, mobile phone plans with different performance options, different sales packages, and different opportunities for integrating other products create an element of confusion that requires greater consideration compared with the purchase decision for a new toaster. The buying decision becomes even more difficult if the customer has little or no experience with this kind of decision.

19. Will the degree of complexity in learning how to use or consume my idea be . . .

    a)   very low – no learning is needed?
    b)   low – minimal learning is needed?
    c)   moderate – normal instruction is enough for most users?
    d)   high – detailed instruction is required?
    e)   Very high – expensive and/or time-consuming instruction is required?

Distribution

Gaining access to distribution is an important part of achieving market acceptance. You can distribute either directly to customers or through intermediaries. The right choice depends on the nature of the idea, the size and proximity of the market, the bargaining power of intermediaries, and the costs involved. There are a variety of distribution methods, and the objective is to identify the one that best matches your intended customers.

If you are targeting a niche market in which customers are concentrated geographically, then direct distribution is a good option because you don't need intermediaries. A product or service that requires ongoing support is also a good candidate for direct distribution because it maintains the link with customers. Alternatively, there may be intermediaries that are able to add value through physical distribution, promotional programmes, or extra services. For example, a weight loss programme based on a meal replacement product used pharmacies as a distribution channel. It was easier and less expensive to reach customers this way than trying to create a network of weight-loss centres from scratch. Moreover, the pharmacists had knowledge of health and wellbeing issues, and customers were comfortable about asking them for information and advice.

Choosing and organising a distribution method involves a number of important questions. Exactly where will customers expect to find a product or service? Who in the existing distribution channels is already dealing with these customers? How many stages must it go through before it gets to the end user? What sort of mark-ups will need to be given away at each stage, and will there be enough profit left over? How much technical support, promotion, or training needs to be provided?

20. Will the distribution method for my idea be . . .

    a)   very simple and inexpensive?
    b)   moderately simple and inexpensive?
    c)   about average in effort and cost?
    d)   moderately complicated and/or costly?
    e)   highly complicated and/or costly?

Market strength

A new idea not only needs to gain market acceptance, but it also needs strength in a crowded market environment. Differentiation and value are the two most important drivers underpinning market strength. Negotiating power with customers and suppliers also determines how securely an idea can be entrenched in the marketplace. And the capacity to stand up to direct and indirect competition makes a crucial difference to long-term success.

Differentiation

Differentiation is the way in which an idea offers features, benefits, or performance that satisfy a need or solve a problem better than the alternatives. A distribution method that gives customers easier, more convenient, less disruptive, or less time-consuming access to an idea will also differentiate it from competitors. Clear-cut differentiation means an idea is not only different but also superior in some way (better, faster, cheaper, etc.) to whatever is currently offered. There are a number of ways in which differentiation can be achieved.

- Features – supplementing basic functions or offering optional extras.
- Quality– better quality at an equivalent price.
- Performance – better performance at an equivalent price.
- Compliance – meeting or exceeding the standards required.
- Durability – lasting longer than equivalent products or services.
- Reliability – consistently performing according to expectations.
- Repairability – easier to fix or obtain replacement parts.
- Style – superior look and feel including packaging.
- Service – exceptional speed, accuracy, care, or responsibility.
- Simplicity – ease of purchase, installation, or use.

Little or no differentiation means that an idea is not likely to fulfil its purpose any better than the alternatives. The vast majority of undifferentiated or 'me too' ideas fail, especially when they can be easily compared with the alternatives. These ideas end up being like commodities in which customers don't care which one they buy as long as they get the lowest price.

21. Compared with the alternatives, will customers consider the features and benefits of my idea to be . . .

  a) very superior?
  b) superior?
  c) not noticeably better or worse?
  d) inferior?
  e) very inferior?

Value

Value means getting the same benefits at a lower cost or greater benefits at the same cost. However, cost is not just the price but also non-financial costs such as wasted time, confusion, inconvenience, or the uncertainty of making a mistake. Benefits are solutions to problems such as saving money, ease of use, superior quality, more pleasure, improved health, more fun, or greater convenience. Some ideas represent *functional value* because they solve material problems and provide tangible benefits. Some ideas represent *symbolic value* by enhancing a person's self-image or social connections. And some ideas represent *experiential value* by providing sensory or mental stimulation.

It is a mistake to believe that an idea will be widely adopted if only the price is low enough. The goal is to plan an idea around the features and benefits that customers value most so the product or service becomes the 'go to' solution for their problem. Research has shown the following to be the top value drivers.

- Differentiation – make sure the value you add through differentiation represents the value customers want to buy.

- Service – genuine customer service is so uncommon that customers will pay extra for it.
- Quality – customers expect quality, but the reality is often not fulfilled. Design quality into your operation and exploit it in your marketing.
- Convenience – what can you do to make your idea easily accessible? Look for ways in which you can make doing business with you effortless.
- Responsiveness – don't make customers wait whether it is in a queue, on hold, online, or on back order.
- Technology – technology can be your partner in business. Look for tools that increase responsiveness, add convenience, increase productivity, and enable you to deliver exceptional customer service.

22. Compared with the alternatives, will customers consider the value of my idea to be . . .

    a)   much higher?
    b)   higher?
    c)   about the same?
    d)   lower?
    e)   much lower?

Customers

Not all customers are good customers. Customers who are in a strong position to negotiate for a lower price or for more features at the same price diminish the market strength of an idea. Price concessions decrease revenue, more features increase costs, and both have the effect of reducing profits. If the customer's negotiating power is not strong, then an idea has greater market strength. Consider the following situations to decide if customer negotiating power is going to be an issue.

- Competitors – if you have many competitors, expect pressure from customers to reduce prices or offer additional services. If there are few competitors, there will not be the same pressure.
- Relative importance – customers will negotiate harder if the cost represents a significant part of their spending or if it is of strategic importance. If it is not, then they are not going to invest as much time and effort trying to negotiate.
- Differentiation – if an idea is not different from the alternatives, or if customers are not concerned about differences in features or quality, then they will buy from any seller and insist on price concessions. If an idea is unique and represents genuine value, then customers will have no alternative.
- Switching costs – customers who can switch suppliers without incurring extra costs have greater negotiating power. High switching costs make it expensive to switch away from you once they are your customer.

- Information – the more information customers have about competitive prices, costs, and features, the greater their negotiating power. The less information they have, the less negotiating power they can exert.

23. Will the vulnerability of my idea to the negotiating power of customers be . . .

   a) very low – no alternatives or no incentive to negotiate?
   b) low – limited alternatives or limited incentive to negotiate?
   c) moderate – some alternatives or some incentive to negotiate?
   d) high – many alternatives or strong incentive to negotiate?
   e) very high – variety of alternatives or very strong incentive to negotiate?

Suppliers

Not all suppliers are good suppliers. Suppliers who are in a strong position to dictate the price, quality, or availability of the inputs you need for an idea diminish its market strength. If their negotiating power is not strong, then you have greater control over the cost and availability of inputs. Consider the following situations to decide if supplier negotiating power is going to be an issue.

- Suppliers – if there are only a few suppliers, then they will have greater power to increase prices or decrease quality and ancillary services. If there are many suppliers or the source of supply is fragmented, then it will be easier to negotiate.
- Alternatives – suppliers have greater negotiating power if the product or service they provide is highly differentiated, if quality is crucial, or there are no suitable substitutes. You have greater negotiating power if what you need is essentially a commodity for which there are many alternatives or substitutes.
- Switching costs – a supplier has greater negotiating power if it is costly for you to switch to another supplier. You have greater negotiating power if switching suppliers can be done without much extra cost or inconvenience.
- Information – the less information you have about competitive prices, costs, and features, the more negotiating power your supplier will have. If you have more information, then you will have greater negotiating power.

24. Will the vulnerability of my idea to the negotiating power of key suppliers be . . .

   a) very low – supply is widely available and pricing is very negotiable?
   b) low – supply is generally available and pricing is usually negotiable?
   c) moderate – supply is sometimes limited, and pricing is not always negotiable?
   d) high – supply is frequently limited and pricing is rarely negotiable?
   e) very high – sole source of supply and pricing is never negotiable?

Competitors

There is rarely an idea for which there will be no competitors. If you believe there are no competitors, then ask yourself why no one else has bothered to pursue the idea. Direct competitors sell the same or similar products or services, and indirect competitors sell something that acts as a substitute. The objective is to identify who the potential competitors may be, determine what threats they pose, and find out as much as possible about their strengths and weaknesses. Irrespective of whether competition is direct or indirect, it will generally tend to be more intense if:

- There are many equally positioned competitors chasing the same customers.
- Competitors have essentially the same marketing strategy.
- There is not much differentiation between competitors' products or services.
- Switching costs for customers are low.
- There is not much growth in the market, and the growth of one competitor can only come at the expense of another.

25. Will the vulnerability of my idea to competitors be . . .

    a) very low – no apparent competitors?
    b) low – one or two competitors?
    c) moderate – a few competitors?
    d) high – several competitors?
    e) very high – many competitors?

Feedback

The purpose of these questions is to identify and evaluate evidence that a target market for an idea can be captured. The issue is not just about the idea itself but also the market you want it to enter. The bottom line is that some markets are just not worth it, no matter how good the idea may appear to be. We are looking for evidence of good prospects for anticipated demand, market acceptance, and market strength. Reflect on the responses you have chosen for each of the questions and how they lead you to a judgement about whether or not the market for an idea can be captured. The responses for market capture will also become part of the Commercial Feasibility Rating in the Appendix.

Anticipated demand examines market size, market growth, market stability, commercial lifespan, and spinoffs. Market size, growth, and stability are of most importance. Commercial lifespans and spinoffs add extra dimensions to demand. Questions for which the response is 'a' or 'b' are favourable. A 'c' response may be tolerable, but it is weak. Questions for which 'd' or 'e' is the response are not encouraging and should be regarded as a red flag about whether or not there is a satisfactory market in which to launch a business.

Market acceptance examines need, recognition, compatibility, complexity, and distribution. Questions for which the response is 'a' or 'b' are favourable, A 'c' response may be tolerable but it is weak. Questions for which 'd' or 'e' is the response are not encouraging and should be regarded as a red flag about whether or not customers and/or distributors will be interested in adopting the proposed product or service.

Market strength examines differentiation, value, customers, suppliers, and competitors. The questions for differentiation and value are critical and we are looking for 'a' or 'b' responses. Questions for which responses are 'a' or 'b' are favourable. A 'c' response is marginal. Questions for which 'd' or 'e' is the response are not encouraging and should be regarded as a red flag about whether or not the idea has enough strength to capture its market.

Part C

Unlocking an operating strategy

The ways in which businesses operate vary tremendously. Some sell a product with accompanying services in order to enhance the product's appeal like a personal computer retailer. Some sell a service with accompanying products to enhance the appeal of the service like a beautician. Some sell a pure service such as child minding. Even a pure service business, however, can be equipment-intensive or people-intensive. Online operations can take place exclusively on the Internet, and they are capable of enhancing traditional businesses as well.

Chapter 7 examines operations in a service business. It includes the diversity of service businesses, the factors driving growth in services, how to promote a service, unique challenges in providing services, and a special section on hospitality operations in the aftermath of the pandemic.

Chapter 8 focuses on operations in an online business, including 'pure click' businesses and 'brick and click' businesses. These include virtual marketplaces, online merchant operations, how to get a website up and running, and how to promote it. The chapter concludes with a description of online operations using mobile devices.

Chapter 9 describes operations in a retail business. These include the effects of disruption and innovation in retailing, choosing a location, negotiating a lease, designing the interior of the selling space, and managing the retail operating cycle. The chapter concludes with an introduction to point-of-sale technology.

Chapter 10 considers operations in a manufacturing business including a framework for selecting a location, designing the layout, production scheduling, outsourcing, stock control, and distribution.

At the end of Part C, there is a reality check in which a series of questions is used to identify and evaluate the expertise and resources that underpin an operating strategy. Expertise includes marketing, technical, financial, operational, and managerial skills and experience. Resources include financial resources, physical resources, human resources, critical information, and access to help and assistance. Together they provide an insight into any constraints that may affect the feasibility of an operating strategy.

DOI: 10.4324/9781003394808-12

7 Service operations

A service business performs a task for the customer that generally requires specialised training, experience, or equipment. Some service operations are focused on the person performing the service (such as a handyman, massage therapist, or consultant) while others are focused on the specialised equipment used to deliver the service (such as a dry cleaner, fitness centre, or car wash). Service businesses tend to be local, and they seldom have to contend with the national or international organisations that are found in retailing and manufacturing. Many service operations can be launched with less investment than is needed to start a retail or manufacturing business. Some service operators are able to begin at home, thus avoiding the cost of premises. Services like bookkeeping, house painting, lawn care, housekeeping, and tutoring, can be launched with a modest investment. Others require an investment in facilities or equipment such as holiday accommodation, restaurant fit out, laundromat, or childcare facility. The purpose of this chapter is to describe important elements of service business operations.

Diversity and growth in services

There is considerable diversity within the services sector and the ways in which businesses operate. Some are focused on providing services to individual consumers, and others provide services to other businesses and government organisations. Here are some examples.

- Personal services – such as pet grooming, beautician, hairdresser, seamstress, photography studio, realtor, wedding planner, marriage counsellor, weight loss adviser, and childcare.
- Business services – such as advertising, bookkeeping, mailing services, computer services, consulting, training, and recruiting.
- Maintenance services – such as cleaning, garden maintenance, plumbing, electrical, appliances, and automobiles.
- Food and beverage services – such as fine dining, casual dining, ethnic restaurants, cafes, takeaways, pubs, and catering.

DOI: 10.4324/9781003394808-13

- Accommodation – such as a boutique hotel, motel, bed and breakfast, short term rental, hostel, and caravan park.
- Transportation services – such as a truck, bus, taxi, limousine, ride share, and car rental.

Changes in Australia's social structure and standard of living have contributed to a surge in service business start-ups. As living standards improved, consumers began to purchase services such as garden maintenance and house painting that they previously did themselves. More free time and increased wealth have resulted in greater demand for leisure services such as travel agencies, hospitality services, golf courses, and guided tours. Increasing numbers of women have entered the work force, resulting in greater demand for services such as childcare and house cleaning. The ageing population has increased the demand for services in health care and aged care. These have collectively contributed to robust growth in services and abundant opportunities for aspiring small business operators.

Service businesses offer the advantage of a flexible operation because you can choose to work part-time, full-time, or seasonally. The first option is to offer services on a part-time basis. If the objective is simply to generate extra income, then offering services part-time is an ideal choice. If the ultimate goal is a full-time business, starting out part-time is a good way to make sure it is something you enjoy and want to pursue. One big advantage of starting off part-time is the opportunity to stay in a job while building the business.

Starting out full-time may be more appealing if you are not currently in a job and you are confident about operating your own business. You will need enough money to support yourself until it becomes profitable. Another option is to offer services during part of the year. Most seasonal businesses operate full-time during the season. Examples of seasonal businesses include income tax preparation, summer camp counsellor, tour guide, or ski instructor.

Service businesses tend to follow one of three operating strategies. *Standardisation* is an operating strategy that minimises costs, maximises productivity, and produces a uniform service. An automatic car wash is an example. *Flexibility* is an operating strategy aimed at providing a broad range of customised services. An interior decorator is an example. *Penetration* is an operating strategy designed to offer a variety of services to the same customers. For example, a lawn care business may offer hedge trimming and weeding in addition to lawn mowing.

Success in a service operation depends on two kinds of expertise. The first is expertise in delivering the service. Customers expect a service provider to have in-depth knowledge about the service and the technical competence to deliver it. The second is expertise in promoting services. Promoting a service is different from promoting a product because the intangible nature of a service presents unique challenges in terms of customer expectations, competition, and pricing.

Promoting services

Service customers typically need lots of information before they will pay for a service. They need to know why they need the service, how it works, and why you are the best one to deliver it. There are many ways to promote a service business, and the key is to select the ones that fit the services you offer.

Print business cards and stationery. These tell existing and prospective customers that you take your business seriously. Business cards are still one of the best marketing tools around for a service business. You can have them printed relatively inexpensively, and you should give them out liberally. If you have a website, be sure to put your website address on your business card, letterhead, and any handouts you produce.

Ask for referrals. One of the best ways to promote a service is through word of mouth. A happy customer will typically want to share their experience and tell people why they liked the service. Some service providers use referral programmes as an integral part of promoting their business by offering customers a free service for sending a referral.

Check out traditional marketing media. Household and personal service providers regularly advertise in local newspaper classifieds to maintain visibility. The key is repetition, and the goal is to get prospective customers to call you or visit your website. An alternative is direct mail or letterbox leaflets. If you have a vehicle, have your business name and contact information professionally painted on the side.

List on online directories. The traditional print version of the Yellow Pages has largely been replaced with online directories such as Yelp, True local, Yellow Pages Online, Hotfrog, and others. If you are not there, then potential customers cannot find you. An online directory listing is designed to get people to call you on the phone or visit your website if you have one. They have already decided to buy, and they are looking for a provider.

Send promotional emails to your existing customers. This is an excellent way to remind existing customers about your services through newsletters and promotional offers. However, emails are not equally effective in bringing in new customers because of the increasing hostility to spam. Be sure to ask for permission before you send someone promotional emails. One way to build a permission-based email list is to ask your customers if they would like to receive free updates related to your services. Email is a relatively inexpensive medium. It can be a great way to keep your business name out there, and it gives satisfied customers something they can forward to others.

Use the power of social media. Put your business profile or page on social media sites that are appropriate for your business. Be sure your profile includes a good description, keywords, and a link to your website if you have one. You can put customer testimonials and case histories on your page and run contests offering a prize or a free service. Place Facebook *Like* buttons on your website pages to encourage visitors to share what they find with friends. Send Twitter messages that give customers free tips. For example, a gardening service might tweet, 'Watering your lawn every day isn't necessary. Once a week for 30 minutes is all you need.' Social media is the digital equivalent of word-of-mouth recommendations. It is an inexpensive way for smaller service providers with few advertising dollars to make a big impact.

Consider setting up a website. If you cannot afford to have someone design and install your website, you can still put one up yourself using one of the templates and tools that make it relatively easy. Then you need to enter listings for your website in search engine directories. Google and Bing both offer free listings for local businesses.

Run information sessions and demonstrations. The key is to focus on the benefits of using your service rather than its features or prices. Free demonstrations are another way to encourage potential customers to try a service. For example, if you offer personal training, you might give a presentation and a free exercise session to groups of potential customers.

Unique challenges

Services pose unique challenges when they are produced and consumed in the presence of a customer. The customer may not have an opportunity to evaluate the service prior to purchase, leading to potential dissatisfaction if they receive something that is different from what they expected. It may also be difficult to detect and remedy errors before the customer sees them. If the customer actively participates in delivering the service, such as aerobic exercise instruction, the quality of the service depends on the customer's contribution as well.

Unlike physical goods, services cannot be put into inventory for future use. For example, when a bus drives off with empty seats the revenue is lost forever. Revenue is also lost if the demand for services exceeds the capacity to serve customers. Because service businesses have no inventories with which to smooth out these imbalances, they need to pay careful attention to matching the timing of supply and demand.

Services are also variable in the sense that the same service is not always delivered in exactly the same way, such as a re-upholstering service that varies with each piece of furniture. The more labour-intensive it is, the more variable a service becomes. The variability of a service can play havoc with customers' expectations if they don't know what to expect in the first place. Variable services also lead to inefficiencies such as having to do some things over, wasting materials, and spending too much time on some jobs.

Competition

Some service businesses compete directly with other service businesses such as an accountant, dry cleaner, or hairdresser. Some service businesses compete indirectly with unrelated businesses such as a cinema competing with movie downloads for entertainment revenue. Some retail and manufacturing businesses offer services as an addition to their products such as installation and repairs. Some service businesses have to compete against government agencies that offer similar services such as elder care.

New customers rely on your image, reputation, and word-of-mouth recommendations to decide if they will buy from you. Repeat customers rely on past experience to decide if they will buy from you again. Unlike tangible goods, competing services are not likely to be found sitting together on a retailer's shelf. This means it takes more effort for a customer to compare services and service providers. Therefore, a key element in service operations is a continuous marketing effort designed to encourage new customers to try your services and remind existing customers about what you offer and why they should buy from you again.

Customers are sometimes inclined to provide their own services. Lawn care, home maintenance, tax preparation, childcare, and food preparation are examples. Similarly, business customers might prefer to do their own office cleaning, market research, or deliveries. Customers who want to provide their own services represent formidable competition for a service business. Successfully competing with do-it-yourself customers means understanding why they choose to perform these tasks themselves and then positioning your service so that your package of costs and benefits is more appealing. The obvious opportunities are providing services that do-it-yourself customers don't want to do, or don't have the time, skills, space, equipment, or the know-how. Similarly, you can provide a service that is safer, quicker, and more convenient than what they can provide for themselves.

Service business start-up costs are comparatively low. However, low start-up costs also attract poorly qualified operators. This churn of competitors who continuously come and go from some service sectors makes for a chaotic and testing competitive environment for genuine service businesses.

Pricing

The two most common approaches to pricing services are cost-plus pricing and going-rate pricing. Cost-plus pricing starts by calculating the total cost of providing the service including the materials cost, labour cost, and overhead cost. When you know the total cost to provide a service, mark it up to ensure that you are setting a price that will achieve a profit. This is your floor price for providing this service. If you go below this price, you will be cutting into your profits. If you go below your total cost, you will be operating at a loss.

Going rate pricing depends on what customers will pay for a service. The most important factor is not how much time you spend providing it, but rather their perception of what the service and your expertise are worth to them. There is no magic formula for estimating how much customers think your service is worth. It is something you will discover by trial and error. Find out what competitors are charging for similar services but try not to compete on price if you can avoid it. Instead, try to compete on the basis of your unique service, superior quality, and other factors that set you apart.

You have a choice between charging by the hour or charging by the job. Sometimes this will be determined by whatever is customary for a particular type of service. Pricing services on an hourly basis ensures that you are achieving a return on the amount of time it takes to provide your service. However, customers who want to know the cost of your service in advance will insist on a price for the job. It is important to have a standard pricing policy for services in order to avoid unnecessary customer squabbles over price. Nothing destroys a service business faster than customers discovering they paid different prices for the same service. Wherever possible, published prices should be used to calculate your charges. Even if customers believe the prices are high, they find comfort in the fact that they are being charged the same price as everyone else for the same service.

Some service businesses don't lend themselves to standardised pricing because there is considerable variation from one job to another. In these cases, you need to evaluate each job individually and prepare a quote or bid price. The trick to bidding is to prepare your bid based solely on the nature of the job and not according to what you think your competitors might bid. Each job needs an examination of all the factors that might affect the cost of doing it. Winning a bid that results in a loss is no win at all.

Hospitality services

Hospitality is part of the services sector. The defining difference is that hospitality is focused on enjoyment and experiences as opposed to more essential needs. It is also connected to travel and tourism by providing services for people who travel away from home. The hospitality sector contains a range of small businesses. Food and beverage businesses include restaurants, takeaways, cafes, pubs, and catering. Accommodation businesses include boutique hotels, motels, bed and breakfasts, short-term rentals, hostels, and caravan parks. Travel and tourism businesses include travel agents, tour operators, and tourist attractions.

The hospitality sector was seriously damaged by the fallout from the pandemic. When the ships stopped cruising, the airlines stopped flying, and the states and territories closed their borders, travel and tourism suddenly dried up. When the social distancing and self-isolation restrictions took effect, food and beverage businesses had to close their doors to all but takeaway customers, and accommodation businesses faced massive vacancies. Hospitality is a challenging industry at the best of times, and these were not the best of times.

Hospitality spending is discretionary spending, and consumer confidence is what drives discretionary spending. The more people are confident about the future, the more they are willing to spend. Let's have a look at the hospitality sector with a view to identifying practices that underpin successful operations.

Food and beverage operations

There are two ways to get into the food and beverage business. The first way is to buy an established operation in which you will immediately have existing customers, suppliers, staff, and cash flow. The downside is that you risk buying a business that may not be performing or may need extensive improvements. The second way is to start from scratch and establish a 'new' venue, having complete control over the choice of location, fit out, branding, staff, and suppliers. Starting from scratch is riskier because you need to find premises, buy equipment, hire staff, find suppliers, and start working before the first customer walks through the door. Prior training and experience in food and beverage are absolutely essential. It is also helpful to have a mentor who understands the business and can offer advice, especially in planning and launching the business. There are a variety of food and beverage operations.

- Fine dining restaurants are characterised by trained chefs preparing gourmet dishes that are carefully presented. Meals are brought to the table by experienced servers with sound food and beverage knowledge in an upscale atmosphere.
- Casual restaurants are typically open for all three meals. They offer affordable menu items that span a variety of customer tastes, and they often use a few key ingredients in different ways to offer a variety of dishes.
- Ethnic restaurants typically reflect the owner's cultural identity. While these restaurants are popular with diners who want to experience food from other countries, they are also of interest to those who are looking for the cuisine of their homeland.
- Cafes provide a place in which customers can enjoy light meals and socialise. They are typically more casual than restaurants. Tea rooms and coffee shops offer similar services.
- Takeaways are food outlets that specialise in offering prepared meals that are intended to be eaten elsewhere.
- Pubs offer customers a place to go out, socialise, and enjoy food and beverages. Many also offer night-time and weekend entertainment.
- Catering services provide food that is prepared remotely and delivered and served at another location. Catering also includes vehicles that have been equipped to cook and sell food such as food vans.

Food and beverage management

Food and beverage operations depend on finding the right people, hiring them, training them, and assigning them to the tasks that suit their skills and abilities. Creating the right team, employing them in accordance with legal guidelines, and keeping up with the demands of the business are ongoing challenges. In addition to functional skills such as food and beverage preparation, cash handling, and customer service, consider other attributes as well such as teamwork, attention to detail, and dependability. Advertising in the local newspaper, on social media, or through employment websites are three ways to find staff.

It is a legal requirement in Australia that staff handling food must be trained in basic food safety. In some states, it is also a requirement to have a nominated food safety supervisor who has the correct training and certification. Training can be done in-house, with approved manuals, through classroom training, or online at *foodsafety.com.au*. For information on the requirements for food standards, visit the Food Standards Australia New Zealand (FSANZ) website at *foodstandards.gov.au*. In the post-pandemic era, customers are more sensitive about health and safety and will be likely to avoid establishments that are not rigidly adhering to newly introduced health and safety protocols.

Cost control is an essential element in achieving profitability. The food and beverage sector was already suffering before the pandemic, with massive labour costs, high operating costs, and high rents. Wages, food, and beverages are called *primary costs*, and they need to be carefully controlled. Other costs include rent, utilities, operating supplies, and advertising that vary according to the type of establishment and the location. Most operations have a service activity and a production activity. Controlling the primary costs incurred in each activity is the key to profitability. Many small operators have cut service costs by converting to a delivery-only model in which production is located at a less expensive location.

The digital revolution and technology continue to play an ever-increasing role in the post pandemic food and beverage sector. In the kitchen, temperature sensors and alarms determine when fries are ready and notify kitchen staff. Out front, remote printers or special screens ensure the kitchen is immediately notified when a server rings in a purchase. Wi-Fi enables credit/debit card hand-held devices to be brought directly to the table to process transactions, saving steps back to the serving station. Other trends include automated services that provide restaurants with an online real-time restaurant reservation system, and there are smartphone apps that tell customers what restaurants are nearby.

Food and beverage marketing

The location of a food and beverage operation is typically cited as the most critical factor in success or failure. Do some research to decide which local area makes a good fit for your business. Inspect potential premises in the area so you know what is available and what each one costs. It is important to determine the volume of foot traffic or vehicle traffic, visibility, accessibility, and zoning for each location. Where are suppliers located, are there complementary businesses nearby, and what sort of competitors are already established?

Stay abreast of the food and beverage trends that appeal to your target customers, the prices charged at similar venues, and how you can differentiate your business from the others. Reviews are part of the food and beverage business, and customers share their experiences online at websites like *Yelp.com.au*,

Zomato.com, and *TripAdvisor.com.au*. Word-of-mouth recommendations are the best form of advertising, and they are turbocharged through social media. Customers generally expect you to have an active digital presence, so in most cases, it is essential to have a website.

Accommodation operations

There are three ways to get into an accommodation business. The first way is to lease the premises on which you run the business. Key considerations are making sure you can live with any restrictions in the lease terms and whether you can generate enough revenue to pay the lease and make a profit. The second way is to purchase freehold premises, either as a going concern or with a view to development, in which you run the business. The initial capital costs are greater than that of a leasehold, but you are not restricted by a lease agreement, and there is greater potential for income and capital gains. The third way is to purchase premises and engage a property manager to run the business. You will need to know a few things before you take the plunge, such as the demand for accommodation in the local market, expected rental prices, the best way to manage the property, and how to market the property to prospective guests. There are several types of accommodation operations.

- Boutique hotels are small hotels that are stylish in design and decor and offer a more personalised experience than the big hotel chains. The popularity of boutique hotels has been increasing, and they account for around one-third of the hotel market.
- Motels specialise in overnight accommodation for motorists. Unlike hotels, they typically offer little in the way of additional services or amenities.
- Bed and breakfasts are small establishments that offer overnight stays and breakfast. Most B&B owners live on the premises. Guests are provided with a private room and either a private bathroom or shared bathroom facilities.
- Short-term rentals are privately owned properties such as homes, apartments, cabins, farm stays, and single rooms. Some rent on a nightly basis similar to a hotel room, and others rent weekly. They are typically fully furnished, including access to kitchen and laundry facilities.
- Hostels are a form of communal accommodation in which guests are effectively renting a bed in a shared room. Bathroom and kitchen facilities are also shared. They offer less privacy than other types of accommodation, but they are also less expensive and therefore appeal to budget travellers like backpackers.
- Caravan parks are places where people with a recreational vehicle can stay overnight or longer in allotted spaces. Many also offer camping and on-site cabins. The term *holiday park* is increasingly common with more on-site cabins and higher-quality facilities than a standard caravan park.

Accommodation management

If you manage a property yourself, then you will be able to keep a close eye on the business, ensure a positive customer experience, and control your bookings. There are some challenges in doing it all yourself because you will need to create online listings, take bookings, check-in guests, deal with guest issues, collect money, and organise cleaning and maintenance. This may not be the best option if you live away from the property, don't have the time, or simply prefer not to get involved.

Hiring a property manager can relieve you of things like marketing across different platforms, dealing with guests, and organising cleaning and maintenance. They typically have a basic charge of around 20 per cent of rental revenue plus extra charges for services like call outs. Engaging a property manager might be a good first step if you are starting out, and you can always consider taking it on yourself when you have learned more about the process. Join the Accommodation Association and take advantage of the tools and resources they have available. It is the peak body for the accommodation industry, and you will find their website at *aaoa.com.au.*

Post pandemic customers are increasingly concerned about the standard of cleanliness in their choice of accommodations. Providers need to be sure they have protocols in place that not only comply with industry standards but also address the heightened sensitivities that are now part of gaining consumer confidence. Examples include a buffer between bookings and different versions of 'deep cleaning' using enhanced procedures. These measures enable you to demonstrate that your guests' health and safety are a priority, and they play a role in your marketing as well. Have a rental agreement that your guests accept as part of the booking process that spells out the terms of the rental and avoids misunderstandings including:

Nightly or weekly rate	Additional fees such as cleaning
Check-in and Check-out times	Cancellation policy and refunds
Booking deposit and final payment	Payment terms and method
Security bond and terms	Rules for noise, pets, and smoking

Today's technology enables an accommodation business to be streamlined with online bookings, check-in, housekeeping, maintenance, and payment processing. Visit *capterra.com.au* to see a comprehensive directory of hospitality management software together with links and reviews. Some state and local governments have been enacting ordinances aimed at short-term property owners. It is important to stay informed because it can affect your ability to own and operate a short-term rental. Make sure you are insured. Insurance on holiday or short-term accommodation properties is not the same as home and contents insurance or landlord insurance. There are only a handful of insurance companies that offer cover for holiday accommodation, and they generally require an approved rental agreement with your guests.

Accommodation marketing

Online marketing is the most effective way to attract guests. The most popular websites, known in the industry as online travel agents or OTAs, include **Booking.com, Expedia.com.au, Wotif.com, Airbnb.com.au, Stayz.com.au**, and other niche websites that suit particular types of properties. You pay a commission fee to these online travel agents when they secure a reservation on your behalf. You will also get direct bookings as a result of these sites because visitors can go onto your website or telephone you to make their booking. You can also take bookings through social media such as Facebook and Instagram.

Prospective guests will first see your property online. They may have done a Google search, browsed online travel agents, surfed social media, or looked up your website after receiving a recommendation. They will visit your website to get information and social media websites for reviews. They want to know everything quickly, without having to search endlessly for information, so the design of your website is paramount. Ideally, you will have clearly visible 'book now' buttons, straightforward menus such as 'about us' or 'attractions', a gallery of professional images, and rates and availability all accessible from the home page. If you make it simple, it's more likely they will make a booking.

Guest satisfaction is an essential part of marketing a property. Since most bookings are processed online, glowing reviews are essential to establish credibility. Once you have a booking, it is common for guests to ask all sorts of questions. Where can I park my car? How do I access the Wi-Fi? Where are the good restaurants? Where can I hire a boat? You are in the guest service business, and if you make it a good experience, you increase the odds of getting good reviews. Establish a database of the contact details of previous visitors. Contact them regularly to inform them of new features or special offers. Give them a reason to return such as a complimentary night for another booking.

Summary

Service operations vary considerably including personal services, business services, maintenance services, food and beverage services, accommodation services, and transportation services. A surge in personal service start-ups has been driven by improvements in living standards, greater wealth, more women in the workforce and an ageing population. Service customers typically need more information before they will buy a service, and there are many ways in which to promote a service. Service operators need to be sensitive to the unique challenges resulting from the intangible nature of what they offer and the competitive pressures they face. Pricing is a big issue in service businesses, and it is important to have a standard pricing policy so that customers know what to expect. Hospitality services are a special case because they are more dependent on discretionary spending. Both food and beverage operations and accommodation operations have been affected by the fallout from the pandemic and the ongoing changes in consumer expectations.

8   Online operations

An online operation is either pure-play or brick-and-click. A pure-play operation only uses the Internet to create a business. A brick-and-click operation is one in which a traditional business adds an online capability. The goal of online operations is to turn visitors into customers. To achieve that, you need to provide an online experience that makes it easy for customers to find what they want and complete the purchase.

There are two ways in which to conduct online operations. You can use the services of a virtual marketplace, or you can have a merchant operation on your own website. Some small business operators think they are too busy running their business to spend time thinking about online operations. The learning curve is not as steep as it might first appear, and there are several ways to get help. Begin with a visit to the Australian Small Business Advisory Service Digital Solutions website at *business.gov.au/asbas*.

Virtual marketplaces

Websites such as eBay, Amazon, and Etsy are virtual marketplaces in which large numbers of individuals and businesses contribute to the mix of products on offer. There is more than one operational model for virtual marketplaces, but the most common method consists of a website that displays your wares, collects your orders and payments, forwards the orders to you, tracks delivery, and releases payment to you after deducting a fee. You are generally responsible for maintaining inventories, making deliveries, supplying images and product descriptions, and pricing.

The main reason virtual marketplaces are attractive is because they have a huge volume of traffic compared with what you are likely to attract on your own. Moreover, using a virtual marketplace avoids having to design your own website, engage a hosting service, connect a payment gateway, and set up accounting software. You can switch marketplace providers whenever you wish, and there is nothing to stop you from using more than one provider. Virtual marketplaces charge one or more of a monthly membership fee, a listing fee, a flat fee per sale, or a percentage of each sale.

DOI: 10.4324/9781003394808-14

Before you decide to use a virtual marketplace, evaluate the various fees to make sure you will be profitable. There are a variety of virtual marketplaces, and new ones are always emerging. Here are three leading examples.

Amazon

Not only is Amazon one of the oldest virtual marketplaces, but it is also the biggest giving you worldwide exposure. Amazon has set up warehousing and distribution facilities in Australia that have firmly established it as the top online shopping website and the first choice for many new online operations. Its high standards have made Amazon one of the most trusted marketplaces in the world. If you are a seller without an established brand behind you, Amazon can provide a much-needed boost to your credibility. However, Amazon's fees are also among the highest, meaning you need to decide if the costs are worth the exposure. Amazon stocks and sells a wide range of its own product lines, which means your products could potentially face some stiff competition from Amazon itself. To learn more about becoming an online seller on Amazon, visit their website at *services.amazon.com.au.*

eBay

eBay is the biggest auction site among the virtual marketplaces, and it is one of the easiest platforms to use. Many sellers have seen an item go for twice, even three times its listed price because of a bidding war among eager buyers. Although you will not directly compete with eBay in the same way you could with Amazon, you will almost always be competing with many other sellers. Standing out from the crowd can be difficult if you are offering a common product. On top of eBay's regular fees, there is also a removal fee to take an item off the site. To learn more about selling on eBay, visit their website at *ebay.com.au.*

Etsy

Etsy is the leading virtual marketplace for anything handmade. It has a reputation for being an easy virtual marketplace to use, and unlike eBay and Amazon, Etsy uses a fixed fee model that makes it far easier to keep track of your costs. If what you are selling is not handmade, however, then it will probably not be suitable for Etsy. To learn more about selling your handmade goods on Etsy, visit their website at *etsy.com/au.*

Merchant operations

Merchant operations mean having your own website. An online shopping trip is a lot like a conventional shopping trip. Customers want to browse through your products, put the items they want into a shopping cart, and proceed to the checkout. At the checkout, delivery arrangements and payment are completed. If these steps are smooth and uncomplicated, then customers will find it easy to shop with you. If any part of the process is not easy, such as a confusing payment system or inconvenient shipping options, then customers have a reason to drop out in the middle of the transaction, and you lose the sale. The five uncertainties that affect online shoppers are how to find product information, how to place an order, how to make payment, how delivery will take place, and if they can trust you to have a secure website that protects the privacy of their information.

Finding information

Provide comprehensive product information using photographs, videos, and text to demonstrate product features and benefits. Include independent product reviews by other consumers to build trust and credibility. Product content should include full price information, including delivery charges, as well as details of stock availability.

Placing an order

Make it easy for customers to order directly from your site, but also offer alternatives like phone or fax for people who don't trust online transaction processing. Your website should have a special page for frequently asked questions, and you can offer to respond to enquiries by phone or email. Include your email address, phone number, postal address, and instructions for ordering so that customers don't have to search for a way to contact you.

An online shopping cart enables customers to select items while browsing through your website. It calculates a running total, GST, and shipping costs in addition to collecting customer account and shipping information. A customer knows what is in the cart, and they can remove items or adjust the quantities whenever they wish. When they are finished shopping, they proceed to the checkout and pay for their purchases. Some online payment service providers offer free shopping cart services. If your online payment service does not provide a free shopping cart, there are third-party shopping cart services you can use on your website.

Make the ordering process simple with the minimum number of clicks between order placement and checkout. Design the checkout page so that it does not frustrate shoppers into abandoning their shopping cart before completing the transaction. Show the full cost, including price, taxes, and delivery charges, before requesting payment details. Ask customers for minimal address and payment information, and avoid asking regular customers to supply information they have previously given.

Making payment

Online payment services can either replace or supplement conventional credit card and debit card systems. To offer online payment, you need a merchant account with your bank that accepts online credit card and debit card payments. Online merchant accounts typically incur set-up fees, transaction fees, and account-keeping fees. Having only credit and debit card payment options, however, may turn some customers away, so offer alternative payment methods as well.

For customers who don't want to submit credit card details online, there are secure payment services that act as intermediaries. They enable a customer to pay by credit card or electronic transfer without disclosing their account details. The customer pays the online payment service, which then transfers the funds into your bank account. Examples of online payment services include PayPal, Paymate, and eWay. They typically redirect customers from your website to the payment service website to complete a transaction. Being forced to leave your website can be confusing for some customers, especially those who are new to online shopping, and it could cause them to abandon a transaction.

Another payment method for customers who don't wish to disclose their credit or debit card details is direct debit from their cheque or savings account. The customer transfers money from their bank or credit union account directly into your bank account. *BPAY* is an example of a popular direct payment system. It is important that your customers clearly identify their purchase so you can match it up with their payment. As a last resort, you can always accept a customer's cheque or money order, but make sure it clears before you ship the goods.

Making delivery

Once payment has been made, a purchase can be delivered in a number of ways, depending on the product.

- Downloading – this method is used for digital media products such as software, music, movies, images, or smart phone apps.
- Direct shipping – the product is shipped by you directly to the customer. Shipping costs reduce the price advantage of online merchandise, so many online merchants offer free shipping on sufficiently large orders.
- Drop shipping – the order is passed to the manufacturer or third-party distributor, who ships the item directly to the consumer, bypassing you to save time, money, and space.
- Click and collect – the customer orders online and picks up the product at a local store. This method is often used by brick-and-click retailers.
- Click and deliver – this is the same as click and collect except the product is delivered to the customer.
- Printout – items such as admission tickets, gift certificates, and coupons can be printed on the customer's printer and redeemed in-store or online.

Customers are more confident about making online purchases if you offer online order tracking facilities. See, for example, Australia Post online tracking services at *auspost.com.au*.

Security and privacy

Online customers, especially customers who are new to your website, worry about the security of their private details such as personal particulars, transaction records, and credit card numbers. Not only do you need to take steps to ensure your website is secure, but you also need to explicitly tell visitors to your website exactly what protection is in place. Here are a few examples.

- Authentication is a common security measure that requires a user to provide a username and password to access restricted information.
- Public Key Infrastructure uses data encryption to transmit customer information in a form that cannot be read by another party.
- Firewalls are security systems that protect customers' information from hackers.
- Secure Socket Layer is a secure protocol used to transmit sensitive information such as a customer's credit card number.
- Certificate Authority is a trusted organisation that issues digital certificates used to confirm a party's identity.

Privacy is not just about having a secure website. Customers are also concerned about how you intend to use their private information. Tell them you will protect their privacy and explicitly state your privacy policy. For example, you can state that you don't share private information with any other party unless you have the customer's consent.

Registering a domain name

A domain name is a unique name that is used to access your website. All domain names have a domain suffix, such as. com,. net, or. org. The domain suffix identifies the type of website the domain name represents. For example, *.com* domain names are typically used by commercial websites. Australian domain names end with the *.au* country code. For example, the domain name for Telstra is **telstra.com.au**.

Domain names are relatively inexpensive to register, but they must be renewed periodically. Once you decide on a domain name and register it, the name is yours until you stop renewing it. You can register a domain name online. A list of accredited registrars can be found on the auDA website at **auda.org.au**. A domain name that is unique to your business conveys a professional image that is easy for people to remember. Keep your domain name as short as possible and avoid slashes, hyphens, underscores, or anything else that makes it complicated.

Building a website

Once you know what you want your website to do, you need to consider how you will get it up and running.

- How will your website be connected to the Internet?
- Who will design and develop your website?

- Who will maintain your website, and what does that involve?
- Does your website need to accept orders online?
- Does your website need to accept payments online?
- Does the operation of your website need to connect to your order system, inventory system, and accounting system?

Template website design

A website template is a pre-designed set of web pages that you can use to plug in your own content. Website templates enable you to set up your website without having to hire a professional web developer or designer. This is one way to build a reasonably priced website that can be listed in search engines. Website building programs, such as Wix, Weebly, Squarespace, web.com, GoDaddy, and others, allow you to edit your website directly online though a web browser. Although this may be convenient, it can also be time-consuming and you will not have a copy of it anywhere except inside the web builder's program cloud. Content management systems and web builder systems are also offered through many hosting services. When you use the stock website template designs included with a host package, however, you may find it difficult to switch to another host at a later time. Self-contained webpage templates don't have these drawbacks. A stand alone or self-contained website template is a complete website that you download and run independently on your own computer or server.

Custom website design

Hiring a developer will be more costly than using a template. However, a professional designer is experienced in website building and will make effective use of the resources required to build your site. If you decide to hire a custom website designer, start by making an outline of your vision for the website. Writing the page copy and gathering your images before you contact a developer will also speed up the process. Check out your competitors' websites for some ideas as well. The more precisely you outline your needs to the developer, the more time and money you will save.

Choosing a hosting service

The term *hosting service* refers to a business that rents out their computer servers to store your website and connects to the Internet so that customers can access it. There are four main types of web hosting. Each differs in storage capacity, technical knowledge required, speed, and reliability.

- In shared hosting, your website is placed on a server with many other websites, with which you share resources such as storage and processing capacity. The cost is typically low, so most websites with moderate traffic and standard software are typically hosted on this type of server. Shared hosting is also widely accepted as an entry-level hosting option because it requires a minimum of technical knowledge.

- A virtual private server host divides their server into sections in which each website runs as if it were on its own dedicated server. This type of host is for websites that need greater control at the server level but don't want to invest in a dedicated server.
- A dedicated server host offers maximum control in which you exclusively rent an entire server. Your website is the only website stored on the server. Dedicated servers are very expensive, and they are only for those websites that need maximum control and better server performance.
- Cloud hosting offers unlimited ability to handle high traffic or traffic spikes. A group of servers, called a *cloud*, work together to host a group of websites. This allows multiple computers to work together to handle high traffic levels or spikes for any particular website.

If it is your first website, consider starting out small with a shared hosting account. It is the least costly, easy to maintain, and sufficient for most new sites. You can always upgrade to a virtual private server or a dedicated hosting server later if your website needs more capacity. Website building and content management services typically offer web hosting packages as well. A website where you can learn more about hosting services in Australia is Web Hosting Reviews at *webhostingreviews.com.au*.

Promoting a website

It is a mistake to believe that people will automatically be drawn to your website. The reality is that it is increasingly difficult to cut through the sheer volume on the Internet in order to get noticed. Your website needs to generate quality traffic, and that calls for a focused promotional campaign to tell your current and prospective customers how to find you. Drivers of web traffic are search engines, online directories, online promotion, and offline promotion.

Register with search engines

It is essential to be listed in the leading Internet search engines. In Australia, the majority of your traffic is likely to come from Google at *google.com.au,* Bing at *bing.com, and* Yahoo at *au.yahoo.com*. The first option is to list your website yourself. Each search engine has its own guidelines for submission. Generally, you only need to list your home page. The search engine then sends out its automated *spider* to retrieve the other pages of your website and put them in its database. Search engines vary in the depth to which they catalogue pages, so you might want to register all of your important pages separately.

There are alternatives to listing a website yourself. A number of services will submit your website to major search engines and directories. You fill out an online form that includes your site's title, URL, keywords, and other information, and the service handles the submission process. You can also buy Internet promotion software that performs a similar task. While these methods save you time by automating the registration process, they don't give you much flexibility in terms of how you describe your website or which pages you register.

Search engine optimisation (SEO) is a method for obtaining higher-ranking placements in search engine results pages. Each search engine has its own method of ranking websites, and they are somewhat secretive about exactly what criteria they use. Some of the things they check on include:

- Content – this is determined by your website's theme, the text on the page, and the titles and descriptions.
- Performance – how fast is your website, and does it function properly?
- Authority – does your website have good enough content to link to, or do other authoritative sites use your website as a reference?
- User experience – how does the site look? Is it easy to navigate? Does it look safe?
- Bounce rate is the percentage of visitors who leave a site after viewing only one page. A high bounce rate is a sure sign that a website is boring or off-putting.

Optimising your website consists of not only good design principles but also the use of meta tags such as heading tags, title tags, description tags and keyword tags. Unless you are comfortable with this technology and know how to use HyperText Mark-up Language (HTML), it is probably best to engage a website design service to optimise your website.

Online directories

In addition to the top search engines, list your website in directories that fit your business profile. These include industry search websites that focus on businesses in a single market, regional directories that list businesses in a specific geographic area, or trade association websites that have searchable member listings. These listings won't generate the same volume of traffic as the large search engines, but they will give you access to a targeted audience for the products and services you sell. Here are some examples of directories in Australia.

- Google My Business – *google.com/ business/*
- Yelp – *yelp.com.au*
- TrueLocal – *truelocal.com.au*
- Yellow Pages – *yellowpages.com.au*
- StartLocal – *startlocal.com.au*
- Come on Aussie – *directory.coais. com*
- Hotfrog – *hotfrog.com.au*
- AussieWeb – *aussieweb.com.au*

Promoting online

As well as search engine optimisation and online directories, you can use the power of the Internet itself to promote your website. Examples include banner ads, links from other websites, posting announcements on blogs, and publishing a newsletter.

Buying banner ads

Some websites sell advertising banners that will advertise your business and link to your website. Banner advertising gives you creative flexibility in colours, fonts, images, sound, and video. Look for banner ad space on established websites that cater to your target market. Contact the Webmaster at these sites to find out about their ad requirements as well as their costs. In general, banner rates are based on the number of times the ad is served called *impressions*. The amount you pay per thousand impressions is based on the site's ability to deliver a target audience.

Link advertising

The big search engines offer pay per click (PPC) link advertising. Your online ad appears in a sponsored link area when a user searches for particular keywords. You are charged a click-through fee if the user clicks on the ad and jumps to your website. This is a good way to drive traffic to your site. However, the click-through fees can easily mount up, so make sure you are getting traffic that results in sales.

Look at the websites of related businesses to see if they complement yours. If they do, send an email to the Webmaster, and ask them if they would like to include your website on their links page. Offer to reciprocate by placing a link to their website on your links page. Make sure their image corresponds to yours and that you share similar customers. You can also seek links with vendors, suppliers, and providers of complementary products and services. Your goal is not to generate high-volume traffic but high-quality prospects who will be interested in your website.

Post announcements on blogs

Target only those blogs that cover topics associated with your products and services. Provide some useful advice, not just an advertisement, and announce that your website has more information on the same topic.

Publish an e-newsletter

Ask visitors to your website if they would like to sign up for a newsletter that you distribute by email. It can be used to keep visitors up to date about changes to your website as well as information about your products and services.

Promoting offline

Tell everyone, including customers, prospects, suppliers, business associates, and colleagues, that your business is on the Internet. Put your website address on all of your marketing and sales materials including your business cards, stationery, advertisements, brochures, newsletters, and product literature. Anything that normally contains your telephone number should also contain your website address and your email address.

Mobile devices

Mobile devices like smartphones and tablets are rapidly overtaking the number of desktop computers and laptops in use. Having a mobile-friendly website becomes an important part of your online presence. The desktop computer version of a website can be difficult to use on a mobile device if it requires the user to pinch or zoom in order to read the content. Users who find this frustrating are likely to abandon the site. Alternatively, a mobile-friendly version of a website is easy to read and use.

There are two design strategies for building a website that displays well on mobile devices. Responsive website design is the more affordable strategy in which a single version of your website automatically adjusts to display properly on desktops, laptops, tablets, and mobile phones. If you choose a responsive template for your initial website, then becoming mobile friendly is easy.

Alternatively, adaptive website design identifies the user's device and generates a version of the webpage that is matched to its capabilities. Adaptive web design consists of multiple versions of a web page to fit different user devices. It is another way of achieving the same objective as responsive web design, but it is significantly more complex and expensive.

An alternative to a website is mobile application software, usually called an *app*. Apps run on the mobile device itself rather than through a mobile website browser. Web browsing requires a user to launch a web browser, enter a website address, and wait for the site to load. A mobile app launches instantly because the information is stored on the mobile device itself. You can have an app designed especially for your business that customers download onto their mobile device.

Summary

There are two ways to conduct online operations. You can use the services of a virtual marketplace, or you can have a merchant operation on your own website. There is more than one operational model for virtual marketplaces, but the most common method consists of a website that displays your wares, collects your orders and payments, forwards the orders to you, tracks delivery, and releases payment to you after deducting a fee. Examples are Amazon, eBay, and Etsy.

Merchant operations consist of having your own website in which customers browse through your products, put the items they want into a shopping cart, and proceed to the checkout, where delivery arrangements and payment are completed. You can build your own website using a website template such as Wix, Weebly, Squarespace, Web.com, or GoDaddy. The alternative is to hire a web developer to design a custom website and install it on a web hosting service for you.

Your website needs to generate quality traffic, which calls for a focused promotional campaign. Drivers of web traffic are listings on search engines, listings on online directories, online promotion, and offline promotion. Having a mobile-friendly website becomes an important part of your online presence if your customers want to visit your website using a mobile device.

9 Retail operations

Retailing is the sale of goods by a business to a consumer for their own use. Retailers don't usually produce their own goods. They purchase them from a manufacturer or a wholesaler and resell them to consumers. An independent retailer is someone who builds a business from the ground up or buys an existing business and takes over its operation. A large number of retail businesses in Australia are franchises. A franchise is a pre-packaged business with a business plan, a trademarked name, an exclusive product line, and established operating procedures. The trade-off is less freedom to operate like an independent retailer as well as the fees that are payable to the franchise owner.

For decades, brick-and-mortar retailing dominated the small business sector. It enjoyed sustained expansion, which eventually consolidated around a few retail heavyweights and hundreds of franchise organisations, leaving a smaller cohort of independent retailers. Overexpansion finally led to market saturation and incredible competition, reducing the viability of many retailers large and small well before the pandemic crisis.

The interplay between digital technology, changing customer expectations, and new business models has created both opportunities and challenges for retailers. The pandemic experience accelerated changes in the way customers look for information and how they decide what to buy. The traditional retail business model is no longer as robust as it once was, and those retailers who prosper will design their operations to meet these challenges. For up-to-date information and advice about retail operations, you can visit the Australian Retailers Association website at *retail.org.au*, the National Retail Association website at *nra.net.au*, and the National Online Retailers Association website at *nora.org.au*.

Disruption and innovation

Traditional brick-and-mortar retailers were feeling the effects of the digital revolution long before the pandemic. There was plenty of evidence that consumers were switching part of their spending to online, and it was undermining the role of traditional retailers. Nevertheless, there was a lingering reluctance by retailers and consumers to fully embrace online purchasing until the pandemic

DOI: 10.4324/9781003394808-15

abruptly disrupted the retail landscape. Retailers are recognising the need to invest in online operations because customers are shopping less in-store as they become more comfortable with online shopping.

There will always be customers who prefer the touch and feel of a brick-and-mortar retail store. On the other hand, younger customers are more likely to seek and buy products online with a view to in-store pickup or home delivery. In between are consumers who make convenience purchases online but they like to make discretionary and high-end purchases in person. The key to future retailing is to offer a seamless shopping experience, whether a customer is in-store, online, or on a mobile device.

Embracing the technology of e-commerce is more straightforward for franchised retailers because the franchise owner typically sets up a platform that is rolled out across the franchise network. Independent retailers can do it themselves using an online website builder. Unless you have the time and some expertise, however, it is usually less frustrating and more efficient to engage the services of a specialist.

Retail location

Some retail businesses depend on foot traffic and are located within walking distance of the people they serve. Other retail businesses cater to a mobile clientele and can be located some distance from the customer. There are four types of retail trading areas, and each has advantages and disadvantages for different types of retail businesses.

- A wayside area usually appeals to transitory customers. Operating costs are low and so are the rentals. The merchandise is usually of a mixed nature, and there is extensive parking, long hours, and personal service.
- A neighbourhood or suburban shopping area draws local customers. Operating costs are low and so are the rentals. Consisting mostly of smaller businesses, they feature personalised service and plenty of parking.
- A central shopping area draws customers from a wider area. Operating costs are higher and so are the rentals. It is an area of keen competition and larger stores.
- A shopping centre is different from operating on Main Street or in a neighbourhood shopping area. Shopping centres have a distinctive appeal because parking is easy and customers can walk conveniently to a variety of stores. However, operating costs and rentals are much higher as well as intense competition from the 'anchor' stores.

What you sell affects the choice of a retail location. Customers tend to behave differently depending on whether you sell convenience goods, shopping goods, or speciality goods. Convenience goods are usually inexpensive, bought by habit, purchased frequently, and available in many outlets. Examples are milk, newspapers, and confectionery. If you handle convenience goods, the quantity of pedestrian traffic is most important. For example, a corner location that intercepts two distinct traffic flows is usually a better site than one in the middle of the block. Convenience stores are limited in their ability to generate their own traffic, so it is more effective to locate a store within a traffic pattern than to try to generate it yourself.

Shopping goods are usually higher priced, bought infrequently, purchased on the basis of price and feature comparisons, and only available in selected outlets. Examples are clothing, kitchen appliances, and cosmetics. If you handle shopping goods, the quality of pedestrian traffic is most important. Convenience goods are purchased by everyone, but shopping goods are only purchased by certain shoppers and you want to be positioned to intercept them. An excellent site for a shopping goods store is between two high-volume stores where pedestrian traffic flows between them. Another good site is between a parking area and a high-volume retailer.

Speciality goods are usually expensive, bought infrequently, require a special effort on the part of the customer to make the purchase, are not materially affected by substitutes, and are sold in exclusive outlets. Examples are art galleries and quality furniture outlets. Speciality goods are sought out by customers who are typically presold on the product. If you handle speciality goods, you can use a variety of locations because you will generate your own customer traffic. However, speciality stores that are complementary to shopping goods outlets may want to locate near them.

Most of the businesses in a shopping centre are franchises or chain stores. If you want to locate in one, make sure the advantages outweigh the costs. You will be expected to maintain store hours, light the store windows, and use signs in accordance with shopping centre policies including the use of shared facilities such as loading docks. You pay for whatever is needed to prepare your space such as floor coverings, light fixtures, counters, shelves, and whatever decorating needs to be done. Sometimes you install your own air-conditioning and heating units. You may want to seek independent professional advice from people who specialise in shopping centre locations.

Negotiating a lease

The majority of retailers lease their premises rather than tying up capital in land and buildings. State and territory governments have legislated minimum standards for retail tenancy. Ask your state or territory small business agency for a guide that covers leasing in their jurisdiction.

The first step in negotiating a lease is to evaluate the landlord. Talk to other tenants and ask them if the landlord responds to their needs. Does the landlord return calls promptly? Does the landlord send service people when they are needed? Is it necessary to pester the landlord for routine maintenance? Does the landlord just collect the rent and disappear? If you are leasing space in a large, established shopping centre, the landlord is unlikely to be very flexible about the terms and conditions of the lease. In most other circumstances, there is significant scope for negotiation. Ask for a rent-free period while you get established, stepped rental rates that start out low and increase later, and a contribution towards the initial fit out.

A lease is a legal contract. Once you and the landlord enter into a lease, you are both bound by its conditions. Therefore, the lease agreement should contain all of the promises that the landlord has made about repairs, construction and reconstruction, decorating, alteration, and maintenance. Be sure to have your solicitor review the lease before you sign it. There are a number of key lease provisions that you should examine carefully.

Rental payments

Rent can be calculated in a number of ways. It can be a regular fixed rental payment, a base rent with an annual increase determined by movements in the Consumer Price Index, a base rent subject to an annual market review that brings it into line with other rental values, or a base rent plus a percentage of gross sales. A common method is a base rent plus a percentage of gross sales over a base sales target. Suppose the agreed base sales target is $2,000,000 per year and the lease terms are $100,000 per year plus 5 per cent of gross sales over the base sales target. If sales are below $2,000,000, then the rental is $100,000 per year. If, however, sales are $3,000,000, then the annual rental becomes $150,000.

Most lease agreements increase the base rental annually according to a formula or in line with the Consumer Price Index. When the base rental clause provides for annual increases, make sure that there is also a compensatory increase in the base sales target. Try to avoid a lease that is subject to an annual market review. If you are able to negotiate a favourable rental, then you don't want to lose your advantage in the first review. Remember that many lease provisions include additional costs besides the rental. Be sure to identify all of these costs and add them to the rental to find your total cost of occupancy.

Lease term

The term of a lease is the length of time you may occupy the premises. Traditionally, retail leases are offered for terms of three or five years. During the term of the lease, you are liable for the agreed base rental whether your business is operating or not. When the lease term expires, you may not be able to renew or extend it. If you have to move, you will lose the goodwill you have built up in that location.

When you spend money on a shop fitout, you want to know that you can occupy the premises long enough for your investment to pay for itself. On the other hand, you don't want to lock yourself into a long lease in case you need to close down, move, or expand into bigger premises. The solution to this dilemma is to negotiate an option to renew the lease at the end of its term. For example, you may negotiate a three-year term with an option to renew the lease for a further three years. If you exercise the option, you may continue to occupy the premises for another three years. If you don't want to continue in that location, then you can simply let the option lapse. It is also important to have the right to assign the lease if you decide to sell the business.

Permitted uses

Permitted uses define the kinds of business activities that you can undertake. Make sure the permitted uses are stated broadly enough to accommodate any changes that you may decide to make in the way you run the business. Permitted use clauses are usually interpreted strictly, especially in shopping centres that try to maintain a balanced tenant mix. They include a number of restrictions that are designed to prevent a tenant from creating any nuisances, disturbances, or damage. Look for provisions that restrict the hours during which you have access to the building and other provisions that require you to be open for trading during specific times.

Interior layout

The objective of your interior layout is to steer customers around the store so they see and recognise as much of the merchandise as possible. Destination traffic consists of customers who know what they want. Shopping traffic consists of customers who have nothing particular in mind and are usually 'just looking'. Destination traffic moves directly toward what they want, while shopping traffic is more unpredictable. Your job is to control the store traffic so that it not only separates destination and shopping traffic but also encourages the smooth circulation of both groups throughout the store. Here are some examples of interior layout designs.

- A forced-path layout directs customers on a predetermined route through the entire store. They are exposed to all of the merchandise on offer, but it risks irritating destination traffic.
- A grid layout is a familiar, repetitive pattern favoured by chemists and hardware stores in which customers can move quickly through an efficient floor space using standard fixtures and displays. The downside of this layout is the lack of aesthetics and the uninspiring environment often associated with its use.
- A loop layout uses a path to lead customers from the entrance of the store to the checkout area by making the floor path a standout colour, lighting the loop to guide the customer, or using a different floor material to mark the loop.
- A straight layout is simple, is efficient, and helps to pull customers towards the back of the store. Bottle shops, convenience stores, and small markets use the straight design effectively.

- A diagonal layout uses aisles placed at angles to expose merchandise as customers navigate through the space. Small stores can benefit from this space management option, and it is excellent for self-service retailers because it invites more movement and better customer circulation.
- A free flow layout rejects typical design patterns. It is intended that customers will feel less rushed in this environment, the store will look less sterile, and merchandise will be more interesting. The risk is that it may confuse customers and disrupt their flow throughout the space.

Creating a store traffic pattern is an exercise in finding the path of least resistance between the customers and the merchandise. When you design the interior layout of your selling space, keep in mind that this is a highly specialised area of retail marketing. Your trade association, franchise organisation, retail design service, and suppliers of store fittings are generally good sources of information and assistance.

Display

Have you noticed how some retailers make it easy for you to shop while others make it frustrating? How you display your merchandise helps to make sales. Customers must be able to see and identify every item you have for sale at a glance. Merchandise can be displayed according to different criteria such as:

Product lines	Seasonal lines	Advertised lines
Brands	Accessories	Promotional lines
Age groups	Related lines	Impulse lines
Colours	Prices	Style
Sizes	Quality	

Your display space is your most valuable asset. It should be apportioned among your product lines according to their contribution to sales and profits. Your best-selling products deserve the best space compared with the merchandise you keep on display simply to complete the product line. For example, eye-level shelf space is a prime position compared with knee-level shelf space. That is why it is common practice to arrange each product line vertically because most customers scan the shelves horizontally. The vertical arrangement enables customers to scan more product lines quickly. They stop when they see the product line they are looking for, looking up and down to find the brand or model they want.

Signs inside your shop can also be used to promote products as well as guide customers through your selling space. Inside signs can be as big as a banner or as small as a price tag. Big signs convey a high-volume, low-cost image, whereas small, discreet signs tend to convey a more exclusive image. With new techniques in instant printing and computer graphics, inside signs can be colourful and exciting graphic art.

Colour and lighting

How you use colour and lighting forms a symbolic background on which you can express the image and mood of your business. The colour scheme should make it easy for customers to identify your business, and it should complement your other marketing materials. Colour can help create a buying mood by enhancing the feel of your selling space and highlighting the merchandise. Generally, a colour scheme should be subtle and blend well with the store fixtures. Strong contrasts and loud colours on the walls and ceilings may get attention, but they can also overpower the merchandise.

Colour is especially important in motivating customers to buy goods that are fashionable. You may want to feature one colour that is particularly popular, or you may want to highlight a family of colours. Higher priced merchandise is best displayed in more refined colour schemes, such as blues, greens, greys, and black. In general, warm colours stimulate and cool colours relax. Warm colours also tend to make objects look closer than cool colours. Soft pastel shades are always a popular overall store decor, with the subtle use of darker colours for contrast. Light colours add depth to a small space, and dark colours help make a large space look smaller.

Lighting catches the customer's eye and calls attention to the merchandise. The objective is to encourage customers to examine the merchandise and buy it. Good lighting does not call attention to itself. It accents the selling space, makes the merchandise stand out, and brings out the natural colours. Lighting is a blend of art, engineering, and experience. Architects, interior designers, and lighting equipment suppliers are all capable of giving you advice.

Retail operating cycle

Once established, retail operations consist of a systematic approach to making decisions about purchasing, pricing, promotion, and stock control.

Purchasing

Different categories of stock call for their own approach to determining what and how much to buy. Some lines are staples that are always in demand with little change in models or styles. Determining what you need involves looking at your current stock and your current rate of sales. Other lines may be seasonal, perishable, or affected by style changes. For these categories, you have to make risky decisions about which styles to select and how much of each to buy. You don't want to get stuck with a lot of old stock if a particular style is no longer popular or a food item is past its use by date. The goal is to maintain stock at the lowest level possible and still have a sufficient variety of colours, sizes, flavours, or models available.

Find out what lines and quantity discounts are available from all of the vendors and what kind of deals your suppliers have been doing with your competitors. Make the supplier's representatives work for you, even if you are fully prepared to buy from them anyway. Negotiation involves not only the purchase price but also quantities, delivery dates, single or multiple shipments, freight and packing expenses, guarantees on quality, promotion and advertising allowances, returns policies, and special deals.

Pricing

Retailers don't normally face the same pricing dilemmas as other types of businesses. They typically rely on prices that are suggested by their suppliers or by matching the prices charged by competitors for the same merchandise. For some product lines, retailers may choose to engage in more aggressive pricing practices. Chapter 5 on marketing strategy contains more information about pricing.

Promotion

For generations, the basics of retail promotion remained the same. People who wanted to buy something usually went to a store. Customers were able to locate a store through newspaper advertising, Yellow Pages' advertising, or simply scanning the shopping area for a shopfront. However, times have changed dramatically. Not only have traditional marketing methods evolved, but the Internet also has forever changed customers' expectations of retail businesses.

Traditional marketing continues to play an important role in retail advertising and promotion. Print advertising, radio, and television are the media used to inform and remind retail customers about what a retailer is offering. Just because you operate out of a shopfront, however, doesn't mean you cannot also sell your merchandise online. A website can be a valuable marketing tool by providing customers and potential customers with important information and online ordering facilities. A website also represents an opportunity to extend the geographical reach of your business to capture more customers.

Stock control

You need a system for controlling stock to help you order the right quantities and assortments, simplify buying, assist in selecting items for special promotion, and expedite the liquidation of slow-moving items. *Maintained reorder items* are usually of a staple nature and are consistently available from your supplier. They don't change styles or models often, and your stock position can be adjusted gradually. *Maintained selection items* normally come in a variety of styles, colours, or sizes. Whenever an order is placed the entire customer selection needs to be reviewed. These style items require a careful review to select new styles whenever purchases are made. Variations in the stock position need to be corrected before maintained selection items are no longer popular. *Fast-turning selection items* are usually the least predictable but the most profitable. Stock planning for these items needs to be very flexible and set up to change rapidly. Over-buying is costly because mistakes cannot be reduced gradually, and severe price reductions may be necessary to move stock that is no longer popular. There are a number of stock control systems available that monitor your sales and help you decide when and how much to buy.

Point of sale technology

A retail Point of Sale (POS) system, or the checkout, amounts to an electronic cash register. A POS system typically includes a computer, screen, bar code scanner, credit card reader, cash drawer, receipt printer, and customer display. It can also incorporate other devices like weighing scales. Retail POS systems include touch screen technology, and the computer is built into the screen chassis for an all-in-one unit designed to save counter space. POS systems can handle a variety of retail functions including:

Sales	Loyalty programmes
Returns Exchanges	Quantity discounts
Lay-bys	Promotional sales
Gift cards	Manufacturer coupons
Gift registries	Foreign exchange

The back-office functions of a retail POS system are a powerful management tool including purchasing, receiving, inventory control, customer accounts, GST, and profit reporting. Most POS systems include an accounting interface that is used to transfer information into your accounting system. Given the expense involved and the variety of retail POS systems on the market, make sure you understand your current needs as well as your future needs before you buy or lease one. Visit **Capterra.com.au** for a buyer's guide and a directory of the POS packages that are available.

Summary

Digital technology, changing customer expectations, and new business models have created both opportunities and challenges in retailing. A major factor in choosing a retail location is the nature of the business and the amount and type of traffic needed to sustain it. Most retailers lease their premises, and there are a number of important issues in negotiating a lease. The interior layout of retail premises is designed to systematically steer customers around the selling space including the use of displays, colour, and lighting. Once established, retail operations consist of making decisions about what to purchase, what prices to charge, how to promote sales, and how to control stock. Most retailers use point of sale technology to manage retail operations.

10

Manufacturing operations

Australia has a very small manufacturing sector. We are not competitive with offshore manufacturers across a wide range of goods because our wages and other costs are too high. Over the past few decades, we have been making less and less and importing more and more. The pandemic highlighted the vulnerability of our supply chains and our dependence on imported goods. This prompted the Commonwealth government to promise a renewed focus on helping the manufacturing industry find new domestic opportunities for import replacement and export.

Small manufacturers typically depend on a specialised niche market in order to prosper such as children's toys, apparel, food products, furniture, and leather goods. Manufacturing is potentially the most complicated form of small business to undertake. It typically requires up-front investment in manufacturing facilities, specialised equipment, and raw materials or components. Workers with particular skills may also be required. You not only need to coordinate the manufacturing process but also manage the marketing, financial, and staffing functions as well. There are four guiding principles that underpin operating decisions in manufacturing.

- Lowest unit cost by minimising the costs of labour, materials, and overheads.
- Highest quality by making products that meet or exceed design specifications and customer expectations.
- Prompt delivery by minimising the time between receiving an order and making shipment.
- Low investment by minimising the amount of capital invested in space, equipment, and inventories.

Location

Where you locate depends on the size of your operation. If it's very small, perhaps you can start from home, provided there are no zoning restrictions that prevent you from doing so. But in most cases, you will need something that is more suitable for manufacturing. If the business needs to be convenient to your customers, then you are looking for the geographic centre of your market.

DOI: 10.4324/9781003394808-16

If you find it necessary to employ skilled staff, then locating where there are people with the relevant skills may be more important.

What type of transport do you need to get raw materials or components in and finished goods out? If you have low-value-for-weight items, then your location decision may be influenced by transport costs. If you have a high-value-for-weight item, then transport costs will not be as important. However, if your product perishes quickly and needs to be fresh when it is delivered, then you will probably want to locate close to your customers. On the other hand, if your inputs need to be processed quickly while they are still fresh, then you may want to be close to your sources of supply.

Most manufacturing businesses require an industrial power supply. Check with the local electricity distributor about the availability, quality, and reliability of a suitable power supply. Some areas in Australia have problems with the supply of adequate water. If water is important for your business, check with the local water authority about availability, quality, and seasonal or other restrictions. The cost of waste removal and sewage treatment also affects some manufacturing businesses.

The cost of a manufacturing facility consists of the initial cost and the ongoing operating costs. A low-priced facility is not a bargain if high operating costs destroy the initial cost advantage. Therefore, consider the trade-off between the initial expense and the costs of marketing, staff, and transport. You should also consider whether to lease, buy, or build what you need. Will your requirements change in the future? Do you want to commit a large part of your capital to plant and equipment? Can you secure a favourable lease with options that maintain your flexibility?

Layout

The layout of a manufacturing operation is primarily concerned with the efficient flow of production. Designing the layout begins by identifying the functions that will take place and considering the most efficient relationship that each function should have with the others. These functions are generally located in the office, the production and assembly area, and the receiving, shipping, and storage area.

In many manufacturing operations, the reception area is the showplace of the business because this is where a visitor's first impression is established. The reception area, product display area, and offices create an image for the entire operation. A bookkeeping or accounting office needs to be adjacent to the front office, but it doesn't need to be on public display. A production office should be located so that it is in contact with the rest of the manufacturing operation without the need to pass through the front office.

Ideally, raw materials or components are received at one end of the plant, processed or assembled in the production area, and the finished goods are stored and shipped out from the other end. In very small manufacturing operations, this may be difficult to accomplish, or the location of shipping and receiving areas may be dictated by road access or the location of a loading dock. One way to compensate for a single entry/exit point is to create a U-shaped manufacturing layout that brings the product back to the shipping area without having to backtrack.

Production

Different production methods are more suitable for certain types of products, and it's important to choose the most efficient and cost-effective option. Common production methods include job production in which a single individual makes a product from start to finish, batch production in which different people work on each stage of production, and flow production which is a continuous flow of fabrication or assembly through various steps of the production process. What equipment do you need, and how can it be acquired? You can reduce the cost of equipment by hiring it or buying it from suppliers that provide flexible financing options such as leases.

Raw materials or components will be needed, and you want to be sure you have access to them when they are required. There are a number of techniques available to help you determine the quantity needed, how much to order, and how often to reorder. How will you move your raw materials or components into and around your facility? How will you transport your finished products to customers?

In some manufacturing operations, production scheduling amounts to 'When we get the orders, we make the products'. In other firms, it means 'We produce for the season so we have enough stock available when the season starts'. Either way, production scheduling starts with a forecast of sales. How much do you expect to sell? When do you need to make delivery? Forecasting sales is straightforward if you only manufacture against orders or if the demand for your product is stable. In other circumstances, sales forecasts are less predictable and a cause for uncertainty. Production scheduling consists of determining the type and amount of work that needs to be done, scheduling the people to do the work, scheduling the equipment to be used, scheduling the materials needed, and integrating the work, people, equipment, and materials to create a smooth flow of production. You can visit *Capterra.com.au* to see a directory of software packages for managing production scheduling.

Outsourcing

Doing it all on your own is not always the best option. Outsourcing consists of arranging for some work to be performed by another person or business. The main reason for outsourcing is to save money. One of the limitations of being a small manufacturer is that you may not have all of the skills necessary for a particular job. Outsourcing is a way to gain access to people with the right skills without having to hire staff. Outsourcing can also make your operation more flexible by giving you quick access to short-term resources. For example, outsourcing enables you to bid on several jobs at once without worrying about how you will handle all the work if you get them.

Subcontracting is a more formal version of outsourcing. It consists of entering into a contract with another business to perform a service that is part of a bigger job. When you subcontract work, you are still responsible for getting the work done in a manner that is satisfactory to the customer. A common example of subcontracting is in the home construction industry. A general contractor deals with the customer and administers the project. They have the responsibility for organising and coordinating the work of the painters, plumbers, electricians, and carpenters and paying them for their services.

Stock control

The goal of stock control is to provide the maximum service to your customers at the lowest cost to your business. Your aim should be to achieve maximum turnover of stock without running out. The less money and space you tie up in raw materials, components, work-in-progress, and finished goods, the better. Stock control consists of knowing when to order and how much to order. If you keep too few raw materials or components, you run the risk of interruptions to production caused by shortages. If you keep too few finished goods, then you run the risk of losing sales to customers who are unwilling to wait for delivery. On the other hand, if you purchase too many raw materials or produce too many finished goods, then you will have excess stock and incur extra costs. In short, coordinating your purchases of inputs with your production schedule is crucial to a smooth-running operation. The website at **capterra. com.au** also lists stock control software packages for manufacturers.

Distribution

Marketing channels are the means by which manufactured goods make their way to the final customer. The choice of marketing channels is a trade-off between the cost of using intermediaries to achieve wider distribution and the greater control and higher margins of selling direct. Selling direct means you make the goods and sell them directly to the end-users. Selling direct means you retain control over the distribution of your products, and you also keep the full profit margin. The digital revolution has provided a variety of new tools that enable a small manufacturer to sell direct.

An alternative is to sell your products to retailers. The retailers add their margin, and on-sell them to the end-users. This channel is sometimes used by manufacturers that specialise in producing shopping goods such as clothes, shoes, and furniture. In this channel, you no longer have contact with the end user and you share the profit margin with the retailer.

Another alternative is to sell your products to a wholesaler. The wholesaler adds his/her margin and distributes it amongst retailers. The retailers add their margin to the wholesaler's price and on-sell the goods to the end-users.

Using a wholesaler may make sense if you are a high-volume producer and there are many retailers or they are widely spread geographically. The downside is that your margins will be eroded because you are sharing them with two intermediaries.

Summary

Small manufacturers typically gravitate toward specialised niche markets. The keys to succeeding in manufacturing are low unit cost, high quality, prompt delivery, and minimum investment in plant, equipment, and inventory. Manufacturing is perhaps the most complicated type of business operation, and you need to consider a number of important decisions. Among them are where to locate your manufacturing facility, what layout will give you the most efficient flow of production, and how you will go about scheduling the work that needs to be done. Outsourcing or subcontracting some of your work can sometimes offer cost savings, be a way to overcome skills shortages, and increase your flexibility to accept more orders. Manufacturing is not just about production; in order to sell your products, you also need to decide which distribution channels will work best for your business.

Part C

Reality check

What are the operating constraints?

The purpose of these questions is to identify and evaluate any weaknesses in an operating strategy. The focus is on the expertise and resources needed to create a smooth and efficient operation. Expertise includes marketing expertise, technical expertise, financial expertise, functional expertise, and managerial expertise. Resources include financial resources, physical resources, human resources, critical information, and sources of help and assistance. Each question is designed to identify the gap between what you need and what you already have. Select the response that best describes your situation. Your responses will help you form a judgement about whether or not the expertise and resources you need for a viable operation are available. Your responses will also become part of the Commercial Feasibility Rating in the Appendix.

Expertise

The kinds of skills and experience required depend on the sophistication of an idea and the nature of the market it faces. Having a balance of skills and experience is just as important as having deep expertise in particular areas. Determining what skills and experience are important can only be made on a case-by-case basis. The overriding premise is that the circumstances of an idea dictate the marketing, technical, financial, functional, and managerial expertise needed to commercialise it.

Marketing expertise

Marketing is not just about selling. It is a broader way of thinking and acting in which every decision is driven by an intense focus on how to deliver the right benefits to the right customers. Very few ideas get off the ground without marketing expertise. This is particularly true of consumer products that need to be skilfully designed, packaged, promoted, priced, and distributed in order to gain the consumer's attention. If you hear yourself saying, 'I know it will sell,' then take this as a sign that your approach to marketing is not only

DOI: 10.4324/9781003394808-17

naïve but also potentially disastrous. There are a number of potential marketing issues to consider when you take an idea to the marketplace. Here are some examples.

Business location	Product design
Competitor evaluation	Merchandising
Marketing research	Customer service
Marketing strategy	Distribution channels
Product positioning	Packaging and presentation
Retail layout	Direct selling
Pricing and discounts	Advertising and promotion
Credit terms	Internet marketing
Sales forecasting	Supply chain management
Trade shows	Export marketing

If only modest marketing expertise is needed, then perhaps you will be able to develop a marketing strategy and carry it out yourself. Ideas that require a high level of marketing expertise and sophistication are probably best tackled by those who have the skills, experience, and resources. If you need help, look for someone with the kind of marketing expertise you require.

26. Will the gap between what I have and what I need call for . . .

   a)   no additional marketing expertise?
   b)   modest additional marketing expertise?
   c)   moderate additional marketing expertise?
   d)   a high level of additional marketing expertise?
   e)   a very high level of additional marketing expertise?

Technical expertise

An idea needs sufficient technical skills and knowledge to produce and deliver the product or service. Some ideas are straightforward and require very little technical input. However, all products and services require some technical expertise. Ideas that require a very high level of technical expertise are usually best left to those who know what they are doing. It is easy to underestimate the degree of technical sophistication involved in a project, especially if you lack technical expertise or have not been through the commercialisation process before. Ideas that require a high level of technical expertise are occasionally commercialised by very small firms. However, the caveat is that development to the market-ready stage usually requires sustained technical input.

27. Will the gap between what I have and what I need call for . . .

   a)   no additional technical expertise?
   b)   modest additional technical expertise?

c) moderate additional technical expertise?
d) significant additional technical expertise?
e) a very high level of additional technical expertise?

Financial expertise

The primary causes of financial failure are underestimating capital needs and having inadequate control over cash flow. Growth, particularly rapid growth, does not generate capital, it consumes it. Here are some examples of the financial knowledge, skills, and experience that may be needed to put an idea into operation.

Budgeting	Financial statements
Cash flow	Ratio analysis
Breakeven analysis	Debtor control
Banking relationship	Creditor control
Bookkeeping	Cost control
Borrowing money	Payroll
Leasing	Equity capital
Using an accountant	PAYG procedures
Income tax	Goods and Services tax

A modest level of financial expertise is generally enough for small scale operations with little or no financing requirements and a simple accounting system. One way to gain financial expertise quickly is to engage an accountant. Ideas that require a high level of financial expertise need to have greater in-house expertise or outside professional assistance.

28. Will the gap between what I have and what I need call for . . .

a) no additional financial expertise?
b) modest additional financial expertise?
c) moderate additional financial expertise?
d) significant additional financial expertise?
e) a very high level of additional financial expertise?

Functional expertise

Functional expertise underpins the way a business goes about performing its tasks. Some functions consist of repeating a series of relatively straightforward tasks, while others can be highly complicated. Functional expertise also varies tremendously between service-based business ideas, online business ideas, retail businesses ideas, and product-based business ideas. Examples of functions requiring knowledge, skills, or experience include:

Purchasing	Productivity
Stock control	Quality control

Production	Cost control
Service delivery	Scheduling and workflow
Plant and equipment	Transport and freight
Recruitment and selection	Computer systems
Awards	Negotiating
Staff training	Supervising

29. Will the gap between what I have and what I need call for . . .

   a)   no additional functional expertise?
   b)   modest additional functional expertise?
   c)   moderate additional functional expertise?
   d)   significant additional functional expertise?
   e)   a very high level of additional functional expertise?

Managerial expertise

Managerial expertise is different from other skills and experience because the emphasis is on working *on* the business rather than working *in* the business. One of the key lessons in assessing managerial expertise is that the skills, knowledge, and experience needed to manage an ongoing business are generally different from those needed to develop the initial idea. Managerial expertise can be divided into six categories.

* Planning – including strategic planning, resource allocation, and coordination.
* Sales and marketing – including marketing strategy and tactics, sales techniques, and sales control systems.
* Customer service – including assessing customer needs, meeting quality standards, and evaluating customer satisfaction.
* Finance and accounting – including finance and accounting principles and practices, institutional relationships and the analysis and reporting of financial information.
* Legal and governance – including principles of commercial law, government regulations, directors' duties and responsibilities, shareholder agreements, partnership agreements and taxation.
* Human resources – including staff recruitment, selection, training, compensation and benefits, industrial relations, and employee information systems.

It is a rare individual who can lay claim to have mastered all of the knowledge and skills in management. Nevertheless, developing an idea into a successful enterprise means you will necessarily need to master some of them. Perhaps the best attribute of a good manager is the ability to recognise when it is time to bring others into the business with the knowledge and skills that are needed.

30. Will the gap between what I have and what I need call for . . .

    a)   no additional managerial expertise?
    b)   modest additional managerial expertise?
    c)   moderate additional managerial expertise?
    d)   significant additional managerial expertise?
    e)   a very high level of additional managerial expertise?

Resources

When you have access to the right mix of expertise and resources, you are in a position to exploit an idea. Not all resources, however, are strategically important. While common resources are necessary to carry out normal day-to-day business activities, it is critical resources that create commercial traction. Start-ups typically suffer from insufficient resources. The result is that it takes too long to get to market, they perform poorly when they do get to market, and they often fail to capitalise on the full potential of the original idea. The lesson is to avoid wasting resources by carefully concentrating on the issues that give an idea the best chance for success. The purpose of this section is to identify the resources needed to commercialise an idea and distinguish between those that are common and those that are critical.

Financial resources

Having enough money when you start out means more than just being able to open the doors. You also need enough money to cover operations while you wait out the inertia of customers. Customers are creatures of habit, and they are unlikely to change their behaviour immediately just because a new product or service enters the marketplace. Financial resources consist of your savings, your borrowing capacity, and your ability to raise equity. The less money you need to get into the marketplace, the less complicated will be the process of getting started.

31. Will the gap between what I have and what I need call for . . .

    a)   no further financial resources?
    b)   modest additional financial resources?
    c)   moderate additional financial resources?
    d)   significant additional financial resources?
    e)   very significant additional financial resources?

Physical resources

Physical resources are the tangible assets that are needed to operate a business, such as location, premises, and equipment. Many of these are the everyday physical resources that are required to operate most businesses. Critical physical resources, however, are the ones that provide a commercial edge – like the best location, state-of-the-art technology, or access to a limited source of supply. The need for physical resources can be modest for some ideas and substantial for others. Before spending money on plush premises or expensive equipment, consider other approaches to acquiring physical resources. For example, why buy anything new if it can be bought second hand? Why buy anything second hand if it can be rented or leased? Why rent or lease anything if it can be borrowed?

32. Will the gap between what I have and what I need call for . . .

    a)   no further physical resources?
    b)   modest additional physical resources?
    c)   moderate additional physical resources?
    d)   significant additional physical resources?
    e)   very significant additional physical resources?

Human resources

It is one thing to start out in business on your own, but it is quite another thing to become an employer. Before you commit yourself to employing staff, think carefully about the consequences because you will need to devote a great deal of time, effort, and money to address the issues that come with being an employer such as:

Finding skilled staff	Superannuation legislation
Finding reliable staff	Government and union interference
High cost of employing staff	Workers' compensation
Red tape and paperwork	Occupational Health and Safety

You can leverage human resource needs by engaging the services of temporary staff. Another way is outsourcing some of your work to be performed by another person or business

33. Will the gap between what I have and what I need call for . . .

    a)   no further human resources?
    b)   modest additional human resources?
    c)   moderate additional human resources?
    d)   significant additional human resources?
    e)   very significant additional human resources?

Critical information

Having access to information increases your ability to make the best use of financial, physical, and human resources. Although much information is common and easily found, critical information is the key to producing value. Three examples of critical information are market information, creative information, and technical information. Critical market information is a deep understanding of what customers really want and how to deliver better value than competitors can deliver. Critical creative information is an insight into identifying and recombining resources in ways that deliver better value to customers. Critical technical information is know-how that creates value by solving problems.

34. Will the gap between what I have and what I need call for . . .

    a) no additional critical information?
    b) modest additional critical information?
    c) moderate additional critical information?
    d) significant additional critical information?
    e) very significant additional critical information?

Help and assistance

Commercialising a new idea does not mean you are forced to rely entirely on your own skills and experience. There are significant benefits from building a network of organisations and people who have information, knowledge, and expertise that can help you. Initially, the formal part of your network will probably consist of professional advisers, your trade association, and government agencies. You may need to engage a specialist consultant if you need help in solving a tough problem.

35. Will commercialising my idea call for . . .

    a) very little help and assistance?
    b) modest help and assistance?
    c) moderate help and assistance?
    d) significant help and assistance?
    e) very significant help and assistance?

Feedback

The purpose of these questions is to evaluate the feasibility of an operating strategy. The emphasis is on the expertise and resources required to successfully commercialise an idea. If you decide to go ahead, these questions are fundamental to your blueprint for getting started. This is an opportunity to look for anything you can do to strengthen the operating strategy by finding ways to improve some of the responses. These questions will also become part of the Commercial Feasibility Rating in the Appendix.

Depending on the circumstances of an idea, an operating strategy will depend on varying degrees of marketing expertise, technical expertise, financial expertise, operational expertise, and managerial skills and experience. Questions for which the response is 'a' or 'b' are favourable. Depending on the nature of the idea, a 'c' response may also be acceptable. Questions for which 'd' or 'e' is the response are not encouraging and should be regarded as a red flag about whether or not the right expertise is available to commercialise an idea.

Resources are the fundamental building blocks of an operating strategy. They include financial resources, physical resources, human resources, critical information, and sources of help and assistance. Questions for which the response is 'a', 'b' or 'c' are favourable. Questions for which 'd' or 'e' is the response are not encouraging and should be regarded as a red flag about whether or not an important resource is available to commercialise an idea.

Part D

Unlocking a financial strategy

There are all sorts of financial management techniques that have been developed for use in business. However, many of them are neither practical nor useful for a small business. The objective in Part D is to separate what is useful from what is not and present a complete and concise description of how to unlock a financial strategy.

Chapter 11 is devoted to managing money. It demonstrates why profits are not cash and why a profitable business can nevertheless go broke! It argues there is nothing more important than managing your cash flow, and it shows you exactly how to do it. It goes on to explain how accounting systems work, the information in your financial statements, and how to analyse profitability.

Chapter 12 examines how to finance your business and comply with the taxation system. Financing topics include borrowing money, leasing, equity financing, and government grants. Taxation topics include the pay-as-you-go system, goods and services tax, income tax, capital gains tax, fringe benefits tax (FBT), the superannuation guarantee, and state taxes. The chapter also explains what to do if you are subject to a tax audit.

At the end of Part D is a reality check in which a series of questions are used to evaluate the financial projections for transforming an idea into a going concern. It includes questions about expected revenue, investment, financing, profitability, breakeven, and cash flow that together provide an insight into the feasibility of a financial strategy.

DOI: 10.4324/9781003394808-18

11 Money management

Success in business is significantly affected by the financial information you have and how you use it. Without current, reliable financial information at your fingertips, it is difficult to make good commercial decisions. The purpose of this chapter is to describe how to use financial information to manage a business. It explains how to control cash flow, how accounting systems work, the information contained in financial statements, and how to analyse profitability.

Controlling cash flow

If the cash flowing into a business exceeds the cash flowing out, then it can continue to operate. But if the cash flowing out of a business consistently exceeds the cash flowing in, then the business will eventually run out of money and grind to a halt. Small businesses are especially vulnerable to cash flow problems because they not only tend to operate without cash reserves, but they also tend to miss the implications of a cash flow deficit until it is too late.

Profits are not cash

Accounting systems measure profit by matching *revenues* and *expenses*. Unfortunately, the accounting process does not distinguish between financial transactions and cash transactions. To understand how cash flows into and out of your business, you need to be able to match the cash *receipts* and *disbursements*. The following example illustrates why profits are not cash.

You have discovered a fantastic new business opportunity. If you give your customers 30 days' credit on their purchases, sales will be $10,000 in the first month of trading and will double every month thereafter! Your inventory is to be paid for in cash, and it costs 50 per cent of the retail price. Your operating expenses will be 10 per cent of sales revenue and must also be paid in cash. The result is that you will have a net profit margin of 40 per cent, and after four months of trading, your profits will be $60,000.

DOI: 10.4324/9781003394808-19

	Month 1	Month 2	Month 3	Month 4	Total
Revenues	10,000	20,000	40,000	80,000	150,000
Expenses					
Inventory	5,000	10,000	20,000	40,000	75,000
Operating	1,000	2,000	4,000	8,000	15,000
Profit	4,000	8,000	16,000	32,000	**60,000**

Your accountant will be so impressed by your trading results that she will probably double her fees. Your bank manager, however, will not be so impressed. In fact, he will be downright disturbed by what has happened to the balance in your bank account. Remember, your customers don't have to pay for their purchases for 30 days, but you have to pay your expenses immediately. After the same four months of trading, you have a $20,000 overdraft!

	Month 1	Month 2	Month 3	Month 4	Total
Receipts	0	10,000	20,000	40,000	70,000
Disbursements	6,000	12,000	24,000	48,000	90,000
Cash flow	(6,000)	(2,000)	(4,000)	(8,000)	**(20,000)**

How can a business with a $60,000 profit end up with a $20,000 overdraft? The answer is because $80,000 from Month 4 sales revenue is tied up in accounts receivable. Profits are not cash. Without cash flow planning, this profitable operation could easily run out of money and go out of business.

Cash flow budgeting

A controlled cash flow will more than repay the time and effort you give to cash flow budgeting. We shall refer to the cash flow budget for Our Small Business (OSB) during its first year of operation to demonstrate how it works.

Step 1 forecasting sales

Forecasting sales is the first and most important step in cash flow budgeting. Begin by making a physical forecast of sales in terms of the number of units sold, the number of transactions completed, or the number of customers served. Then translate the physical figures into dollar figures according to your expected pricing.

Sales forecasting is always an imprecise exercise, and your actual sales will inevitably be different from your forecast. What you are looking for is a forecast that is within the range of possible outcomes. Of course, the more accurate your sales forecast, the more accurate will be your cash flow budget. OSB's sales forecast is based on estimates of monthly unit sales at an average price of $10.00 and has been divided into cash sales and credit sales.

Our Small business
Cash flow budget
July–December

	Month before start-up	July	Aug	Sept	Oct	Nov	Dec
Sales forecast							
Unit sales		4,000	6,000	7,000	8,000	9,000	12,000
Dollar sales		40,000	60,000	70,000	80,000	90,000	120,000
Cash sales		10,000	15,000	17,500	20,000	22,500	30,000
Credit sales		30,000	45,000	52,500	60,000	67,500	90,000
Receipts							
Cash sales		10,000	15,000	17,500	20,000	22,500	30,000
Collections			15,000	37,500	48,750	56,250	63,750
Term loan	100,000						
Owner's capital	275,000						
Total	375,000	10,000	30,000	55,000	68,750	78,750	93,750
Disbursements							
Purchases	40,000	26,400	39,600	46,200	52,800	59,400	79,200
Wages		2,000	3,000	3,500	4,000	4,500	6,000
Marketing		4,000	6,000	7,000	8,000	9,000	12,000
Interest				5,000			5,000
Fixed operating		5,000	5,000	5,000	5,000	5,000	5,000
Plant and equipment	100,000						
Buildings	150,000						
Land	70,000						
Dividend							
Total	360,000	37,400	53,600	66,700	69,800	77,900	107,200
Net cash flow	15,000	(27,400)	(23,600)	(11,700)	(1,050)	850	(13,450)
Cash position	15,000	(12,400)	(36,000)	(47,700)	(48,750)	(47,900)	(61,350)

Step 2 identifying cash receipts

Operating cash receipts are directly related to the sales forecast. If you sell on a cash basis only, then your operating cash receipts will be the same as your sales. If you sell on credit, however, your operating cash receipts will depend not only on the proportion of credit sales but also on when you collect them from your customers. OSB's cash sales are estimated to be 25 per cent of sales. Credit sales are estimated to be 75 per cent of sales, and they expect their debtors to pay on average in 45 days.

Non-operating cash receipts are associated with one-off transactions such as borrowing money or selling an asset. OSB's cash flow budget shows two non-operating cash receipts in the month before start-up consisting of a $275,000 injection of the owner's start-up capital and a term loan for $100,000.

Our Small Business
Cash flow budget
January–June

	Jan	Feb	Mar	Apr	May	June	Total
Sales forecast							
Unit sales	10,000	9,000	9,000	9,000	9,000	8,000	100,000
Dollar sales	100,000	90,000	90,000	90,000	90,000	80,000	1,000,000
Cash sales	25,000	22,500	22,500	22,500	22,500	20,000	250,000
Credit sales	75,000	67,500	67,500	67,500	67,500	60,000	750,000
Receipts							
Cash sales	25,000	22,500	22,500	22,500	22,500	20,000	250,000
Collections	78,750	82,500	71,250	67,500	67,500	67,500	656,250
Term loan							100,000
Owner's equity							275,000
Total	103,750	105,000	93,750	90,000	90,000	87,500	1,281,250
Disbursements							
Purchases	66,000	59,400	59,400	59,400	59,400	52,800	700,000
Wages	5,000	4,500	4,500	4,500	4,500	4,000	50,000
Marketing	10,000	9,000	9,000	9,000	9,000	9,000	100,000
Interest			5,000			5,000	20,000
Fixed operating	5,000	5,000	5,000	5,000	5,000	6,000	61,000
Plant and equipment							100,000
Buildings							150,000
Land							
Dividend						29,000	29,000
Total	86,000	77,900	82,900	77,900	77,900	104,800	1,280,000
Net cash flow	17,750	27,100	10,850	12,100	12,100	(17,300)	1,250
Cash position	(43,600)	(16,500)	(5,650)	6,450	18,550	1,250	

Step 3 identifying cash disbursements

Cash disbursements can also be operating or non-operating. Operating disbursements consist of two types. *Variable operating disbursements* depend upon forecasted sales. In OSB's cash flow budget, inventory purchases, wages, and marketing are variable operating disbursements. *Fixed operating disbursements* take place regardless of the level of sales. In OSB's cash flow budget, quarterly interest payments of $5,000 are due regardless of the level of sales, and the remaining fixed operating disbursements are lumped together for each month. Depreciation is not included in the cash flow budget because it is not a cash disbursement.

OSB's cash flow budget also has five *non-operating disbursements*. These are one-off transactions consisting of the initial purchase of inventory, plant and equipment, buildings, and land in the month before start-up. There is also a dividend payment at the end of the year.

Step 4 determining net cash flow

This step consists of summarising the cash receipts and cash disbursements to determine their net effect. You can see that OSB had negative net cash flows in the first half of the financial year (except for November) that became positive in the second half of the financial year (except for June). This tells us that OSB needs to make provisions for a cash drain during the first six months of operations and they will have positive cash flow thereafter. At this point, OSB can identify the major consequences of its expected cash flow. If the net cash outflows appear to be excessively heavy, they can examine ways to reschedule or eliminate some disbursements. On the other hand, if they foresee large cash inflows, then they can start to think about building some cash reserves, repaying debt, or perhaps looking for ways to expand the business.

Step 5 determining the future cash position

In this last step, OSB relates the monthly net cash flow to their bank balance. They have $375,000 with which to finance the business in the month before start-up. By tracking their net cash flows, they can estimate their future cash position at the end of each month. OSB is forecast to run out of cash in the very first month of operation and will reach a maximum cash deficit of $61,350 in December. However, the cash flow budget also demonstrates that OSB will generate enough cash flow to repay an overdraft in the second half of the year. This is exactly the information OSB's bank would like to see when they get an application for an overdraft. It tells the bank how much money OSB requires, when it will be needed, and when it will be repaid. Without a cash flow budget, OSB may not foresee the cash deficit that could put them out of business.

Credit cards and cash flow

Credit cards and debit cards are an established way of transacting business. They are also an important tool in cash flow management. When you accept credit card purchases, you don't need to invest cash in accounts receivable, and the costs and risks of credit and collection are practically eliminated. Credit card services, such as *VISA* and *MasterCard*, are available from the trading banks. Receipts from credit card sales are immediately credited to your cheque account as if they were cash sales. The bank assumes the credit risk provided you have followed their instructions. In return for this service, the bank charges a merchant discount fee. The amount of the discount fee is negotiable, and you should shop around for the best deal.

Credit card services are particularly important for businesses with a large number of relatively small accounts. They eliminate the paperwork involved in credit approval, invoice preparation, debtors' records, and collections. They avoid the need to commit cash to debtors and the risk of uncollectable accounts. And don't forget that the availability of instant credit is an indispensable marketing tool. Although credit cards are typically used for retail accounts, they are used for commercial accounts as well.

Accounting system

Ask your accountant for advice when you set up an accounting system. They can tell you which accounting system will suit your operation and what records you need to keep for tax and statutory reporting purposes. Some accounting systems can be done manually, but in most cases, it is easier to use a computer-based system such as MYOB, QuickBooks, or Xero. You can save yourself a lot of unnecessary hassles if the system you use is compatible with the one your accountant uses.

Accounting systems keep track of the property of a business (called *assets*). Then they distinguish between the creditors' claims (called *liabilities*) and the owner's claim (called *owner's equity*). Each of these three categories consists of subdivisions called *accounts*. Activities that affect the property of the firm are called *transactions* and are recorded by noting what property is given up and what property is received. The procedure used to record transactions is called *double entry bookkeeping*.

Accounting systems produce two main financial reports. The first is called the *balance sheet*, and the second is called the *income statement*. Essentially, the balance sheet shows what a business has, what it owes, and the investment of the owners in the business. It can be likened to a snapshot of the financial position of the business at a *point in time*. The income statement is a summary of the financial activity of a business over a *period of time* and the resulting profit or loss.

Balance sheet

The balance sheet is an itemised listing of assets, liabilities, and owner's equity. Here is a description of the Balance Sheet for OSB.

Assets

Assets are what a business owns. They are recorded in descending order of their convertibility into cash. Those that can be converted into cash within one year are called *current assets*. Those that stay in the business for a longer period of time are called *non-current assets*.

Current assets

Lenders and others pay particular attention to current assets because they represent the amount of cash that might be raised quickly to meet financial obligations. OSB's balance sheet contains the following current asset accounts.

- Cash consists of funds immediately available for use without restrictions.
- Accounts receivable are amounts owed to the business by its customers as a result of credit sales.

• Inventory may consist of raw materials, goods in the process of manufacture, and goods held for sale.

Non-current assets

Non-current assets have a relatively long life. In our example, they consist of plants and equipment, buildings, and land. Some non-current assets are subject to depreciation, whereby the original cost is apportioned over their useful lives. On OSB's balance sheet, plant and equipment were acquired one year ago for $100,000. It has a useful life of five years, so each year, one-fifth of its original cost goes into another account called *accumulated depreciation*. After one year, there is $20,000 in accumulated depreciation. The difference between the original cost and the accumulated depreciation is the remaining *book value* for plant and equipment.

Liabilities

Liabilities are debts owed by a business. They are recorded in order of the length of time before they are due. They are claims against the total assets, although they are not usually claims against any specific assets except for mortgages. Liabilities are divided into *current liabilities* and *non-current liabilities*.

OUR SMALL BUSINESS
Balance Sheet
30 June 202X

Current assets		
Cash	1,250	
Accounts receivable	98,750	
Inventory	100,000	200,000
Non-current assets		
Plant and equipment	100,000	
Accumulated depreciation	(20,000)	
Buildings	150,000	
Land	70,000	300,000
TOTAL ASSETS		500,000
Current liabilities		
Accounts payable	73,000	
Provision for taxes	27,000	100,000
Non-current liabilities		
Term loan	100,000	100,000
TOTAL LIABILITIES		200,000
Owner's equity		
Contributed capital	275,000	
Retained earnings	25,000	300,000
TOTAL LIABILITIES AND OWNER'S EQUITY		500,000

Current liabilities

Current liabilities consist of those debts that will fall due within a year. OSB's balance sheet contains the following current liability accounts.

- Accounts payable are amounts owed to vendors and suppliers from whom items have been bought on account and for which payment is expected in less than one year.
- Provision for taxes is the amount of tax owed that is yet to be paid.

Non-current liabilities

Claims from outsiders that come due in more than a year are called non-current liabilities. On OSB's balance sheet, non-current liabilities consist of a term loan.

Owner's equity

Owner's equity consists of the capital contributed by the owners plus any profits that have been retained in the business. Together, they represent the sum due to the owners if the assets were sold for the amounts appearing on the balance sheet and the liabilities were paid off. Owner's equity is essentially a balancing figure in which the owners get whatever is left over after the liability claims have been satisfied.

Income statement

The income statement summarises the activities of a business over a period of time. It reports sales revenue together with the expenses incurred in obtaining the revenue, and it shows the profit or loss resulting from these activities. Here is a description of the Income Statement for OSB.

Sales revenue

The major activity of most businesses is the sale of products and/or services including both cash and credit sales.

Cost of sales

In a retail firm, the cost of sales can be found by adding the amount of purchases to the beginning inventory and subtracting the ending inventory. A service firm typically has a component for wages in addition to materials in their cost of sales. Manufacturing firms typically include some of their overhead costs as well.

Gross profit

The difference between sales and the cost of sales is the gross profit. Gross profit as a percentage of sales is important because it represents the average profit margin on sales before operating expenses.

OUR SMALL BUSINESS
Income Statement
for the year ending 30 June 202X

Sales revenue		1,000,000
Cost of sales		
Beginning inventory	40,000	
Purchases	660,000	
Less ending inventory	(100,000)	600,000
Gross profit		400,000
Operating expenses		
Salaries	35,000	
Wages	50,000	
Marketing	100,000	
Occupancy	45,000	
Administration	40,000	
Depreciation	20,000	
Interest	20,000	310,000
Net profit before tax		90,000
Provision for income tax		27,000
Net profit after tax		63,000

Operating expenses

The other costs of running a business are the operating expenses. OSB's income statement contains the following operating expense accounts.

- Salaries for permanent staff, including the owners, and on-costs such as superannuation contributions.
- Wages for casual and hourly staff including the associated on-costs.
- Marketing expenses such as advertising and promotion.
- Occupancy expenses such as rent, insurance, electricity, and maintenance.
- Administration expenses such as telephone, stationery, postage, accounting, and legal fees.
- Depreciation was first discussed when we described the balance sheet. Although no money changes hands, depreciation is a real expense because it represents an apportionment of the cost of non-current assets.
- Interest payments to lenders but not including principal repayments.

Net profit before tax

When operating expenses have been subtracted from gross profit, the difference is net profit before tax. If the business receives revenue from non-operating sources such as rents, dividends on shares, or interest on money loaned, it is added to net profit before tax at this point. This is the figure on which income tax is calculated.

Provision for income tax

This represents the amount of income tax payable on the net profit before tax. The amount of taxation and how it is paid are affected by whether a business is organised as a proprietorship, a partnership, or a company. In our example, the provision for income tax is also shown as a liability on the balance sheet until it is actually paid.

Net profit after tax

After income tax has been deducted, the last entry is net profit after tax. It is from this amount that dividends or distributions of profits may be made to the owners. Any profits that are not paid out to the owners will be added to retained earnings on the balance sheet.

Analysing profitability

Profitability analysis begins by separating two types of costs in the income statement. *Fixed costs* remain about the same regardless of the level of sales. *Variable costs* fluctuate in proportion to changes in the level of unit sales. In this example, fixed costs include salaries, occupancy, administration, depreciation, and interest expenses because they are not affected by variations in sales. Total fixed costs for OSB are $160,000. Variable costs include the cost of sales, wages, and marketing expenses. When sales are $1,000,000, the variable costs are $750,000, or 75 per cent of sales.

The difference between 100 per cent (of sales) and the rate of variable cost is called the *contribution margin*. OSB's variable costs are 75 per cent of sales, so the contribution margin is 25 per cent of sales. This means that 25 cents of every dollar in sales go towards paying off the fixed costs and then contributes to profit.

Analysis of fixed and variable costs

	Variable costs	Fixed costs	
Sales			1,000,000
Cost of sales	600,000		
Operating expenses			
Salaries	50,000	35,000	
Wages	100,000		
Marketing			
Occupancy		45,000	
Administration		40,000	
Depreciation		20,000	
Interest		20,000	
Total costs	750,000	160,000	910,000
Net profit before tax			90,000

Breakeven point

The breakeven point refers to the level of sales at which a business produces neither a profit nor a loss. The level of sales at which OSB will breakeven can be calculated by dividing the fixed costs by the contribution margin. When sales are below the breakeven point, OSB will operate at a loss. When sales are above the breakeven point, OSB will operate at a profit. The dynamics of breakeven analysis are a powerful tool in making decisions that affect profitability. OSB's breakeven point is

$$\text{Breakeven Point} = \text{Fixed Costs} / \text{Contribution Margin}$$

$$\$160,000 / 25 \text{ per cent} = \$640,000$$

Pricing decisions

OSB is thinking about cutting its price by 10 per cent in an effort to boost sales volume. Currently, sales revenue is $1,000,000, variable cost is $750,000, fixed cost is $160,000, and the breakeven point is $640,000. What level of sales must OSB achieve just to break even at the lower price? A reduction of 10 per cent in the average price will reduce the contribution margin from 25 per cent to 16.66 per cent. With a lower contribution margin of 16.66 per cent, the breakeven point will increase to $960,000.

$$\text{New Breakeven Point} = \text{Fixed Cost} / \text{New Contribution Margin}$$

$$\$160,000 / 16.66 \text{ per cent} = \$960,000$$

A 10 per cent reduction in price increases the breakeven point from $640,000 to $960,000. This is a 50 per cent increase in the breakeven point, and OSB needs to decide if the price reduction is likely to generate enough extra sales to compensate for the higher breakeven point.

Investment decisions

OSB wants to invest in new equipment that will add $40,000 in fixed costs per year. OSB's contribution margin is 25 per cent. What increase in sales is necessary to cover the extra fixed costs?

$$\text{Sales Increase} = \text{Increase in Fixed Costs} / \text{Contribution Margin}$$

$$\$40,000 / 25 \text{ per cent} = \$160,000$$

Increasing fixed costs by $40,000 will require extra sales of $160,000, raising the breakeven point to $800,000. OSB will need to decide if the new equipment is likely to generate enough additional sales to cover the higher breakeven point.

Advertising decisions

OSB wants to place a magazine advertisement that will cost $500 per month. OSB's contribution margin is 25 per cent. What increase in sales must the advertisement generate in order to pay for itself?

Sales Increase = Cost of Advertisement / Contribution Margin

$500 / 25 per cent = $2,000

OSB must generate additional sales of $2,000 to pay for each advertisement. They need to decide if the advertisements are likely to stimulate enough sales to cover the cost and generate an additional profit.

Product line decisions

You can analyse the contribution margin and the dollar contribution for each of your product lines. This will tell you which of your product lines is giving you the greatest *rate* of profit and which is providing the greatest *amount* of profit. Your profits will increase if you concentrate on those product lines with the highest contribution margins. Here is an example.

Product line analysis

Product line	Sales $	Variable cost $	Dollar contribution $	Contribution margin (per cent)
A	500	200	300	60.0
B	1500	800	700	46.7
C	600	600	0	0.0
D	400	500	(100)	(25.0)

Product line A has the greatest contribution margin. Product line B may have a lower contribution margin, but it clearly has a much higher dollar contribution because of its greater sales volume. Profits consist of dollars not percentages. We would be better off if we sold more of product line A because its greater contribution margin would generate a greater dollar contribution as well. Product line C makes no contribution, and we would be better off if we replaced product line C with one that has a positive contribution margin. We would increase profit if we could drop product line D altogether.

Summary

Success in business depends on having current, reliable financial information on which to base our decisions. Small businesses are typically at risk from cash flow problems, and the time and effort you put into cash flow budgeting will help you avoid trouble. Ask your accountant which accounting system will suit your operation and what records you need to keep for tax and reporting purposes. Your principal accounting reports are a balance sheet and an income statement. Knowing your fixed costs and your contribution margin enables you to find your breakeven point. It also enables you to make decisions about pricing, new investment, advertising expenditure, and which product lines to carry.

12 Financing and taxation

Financing and taxation issues occur less frequently than day-to-day money management, but they are nevertheless important. You may need to seek finance to pay for something like buying a business, the fitout of business premises, the latest point-of-sale equipment, or to increase your working capital. Depending on the circumstances, you may want to consider borrowing money, leasing, injecting new equity capital, or applying for a government grant. The taxation system impacts just about every phase of business including the goods and services tax, income tax, capital gains tax, FBT, and superannuation guarantee. The purpose of this chapter is to explain the major sources of finance available and the taxation obligations you will encounter.

Borrowing money

Lenders want to know many things. Are you a good business manager? Are you the sort of person in whom the lender can feel confident? What are you going to do with the money? Will you need the money for a short period of time or for a long period of time? When do you plan to pay it back? How will you generate the money for repayments? Do you have assets that you can offer as security? What is the outlook for your business? Are you likely to be in business for the duration of the loan?

Lenders want to make loans to businesses that are solvent, profitable, and liquid. Your balance sheet, income statement, and cash flow budget are the lender's tools for determining how well you meet these criteria. The balance sheet is used to assess solvency, the income statement is used to assess profitability, and the cash flow budget is used to evaluate liquidity. Submitting regular financial statements over a period of time is the best way to convince a lender of your financial credentials.

Sometimes your signature is all that a lender requires to give you a loan. This might be the case if the lender knows you and the loan is for a short period. However, most lenders require some form of security, particularly for longer-term loans. Whether or not security is required, lenders may want to impose conditions in order to protect themselves against poor business practices. Examples of loan conditions include no further borrowing without the

DOI: 10.4324/9781003394808-20

lender's agreement, maintaining working capital at a prescribed level, carrying adequate insurance, and supplying the lender with regular financial statements. Lenders usually try to match the term of a loan with the useful life of the asset it is financing. This distinction between short-term borrowing and long-term borrowing is an important factor in determining the most suitable type of borrowing.

Short-term borrowing

Short-term borrowing is used to finance assets that turn over quickly such as accounts receivable and inventory. The main types of short-term borrowing are trade credit, overdraft, accounts receivable financing, inventory financing, and bridging finance.

Trade credit

Trade credit occurs when your supplier gives you time to pay for goods after they have been delivered. Essentially, this is an interest-free, short-term loan. Trade credit is the most easily accessible external source of finance. Unlike other sources of finance, it seldom involves complex and time-consuming negotiations, so take full advantage of available payment terms.

Overdraft

An overdraft is an arrangement with your bank in which you borrow through your cheque account up to a certain limit. It may be secured or unsecured. Overdrafts are the most flexible form of short-term finance because you only borrow when the need arises and interest is only charged on the daily balance outstanding. An establishment fee is usually charged by the bank plus a periodic administration charge. Together, these extra charges increase the total cost of an overdraft.

Accounts receivable financing

Accounts receivable lending consists of cash advances equal to a percentage of your eligible customer invoices. The lender takes a registered security over your accounts receivable and will insist that you have proper accounts receivable collection and control procedures. *Factoring* is the cash purchase of your sales invoices at a discount. Generally, you continue to be responsible for any accounts that turn out to be uncollectible.

Inventory financing

Inventory finance, sometimes called *stock finance*, provides funds for the purchase of inventory. Inventory finance contributes to your working capital position by enabling you to purchase stock and make repayments that match your cash flow. This is especially helpful for a business with a big seasonal variation in sales. The term *floor plan* is used to describe inventory finance for businesses that carry expensive items such as cars, trucks, boats, and caravans. Funds are advanced so that the dealer can have a suitable range of units on the showroom floor. The inventory is security for the advance, and it is repaid when the item is sold.

Bridging finance

Bridging finance is money borrowed for a short time until the proceeds from another transaction become available or more permanent financing is arranged. Bridging finance is generally secured, and the interest rate varies depending on the lender.

Long-term borrowing

Long-term borrowing is used to finance non-current assets such as vehicles, equipment, plant, buildings, and property. When it comes to long-term borrowing, the lender looks for assurances that the business will be able to repay the loan out of earnings over the period of the loan. The main types of long-term borrowing for small businesses are personal loans, term loans, and mortgages.

Personal loan

A personal loan is normally used to finance the purchase of consumer goods, but it can also be used to finance a business. For example, a personal loan can be used to pay for a motor vehicle, new shop fixtures, or perhaps the initial inventory. Personal loans are repaid in regular instalments, including principal and interest.

Term loan

Term loans are available for fixed periods of one to ten years. The purposes for which term loans are made include the purchase of a business or investment in fixed assets such as land, buildings, and equipment. They are generally secured and repaid in regular instalments including principal and interest. Sometimes a term loan is *interest only*, requiring only regular interest payments with the principal repayment in a lump sum at the end of the loan period. The interest rate may be fixed or variable.

Mortgage

Mortgages are used to finance the purchase of land and buildings. Mortgage finance is long-term finance, and it is secured by the property it is financing. It is generally repaid in regular instalments including principal and interest. The interest rate may be fixed or variable. It is possible to have second and third mortgages on the same property.

Shop around

The major banks dominate small business lending. The ability to mix both business and personal products is an important feature in selecting a lender. Finding the best deal is a matter of shopping around. Look at the eligibility requirements including the minimum amount you need to borrow to qualify as a business customer. Make sure you know about the account fees, transaction limits, and the discounts offered on lending rates. Examine the personal services offered such as financial planning, share trading, home mortgage, insurance, and superannuation. Consider the convenience of having a local branch versus online banking services. However, be aware that some banks don't handle small business loans in the local branches, so you may find yourself having to deal with someone at head office.

Leasing

Despite many claims about the advantages of leases, they are simply an alternative to borrowing. However, leasing can be an attractive alternative if you don't have the cash to buy something outright. It enables you to regulate your cash flow by having predictable, regular monthly lease payments. Leasing can also help to avoid tying up lines of credit that you may need to finance other parts of the business.

Leasing is always more expensive than buying if you already have the cash to make the purchase. If the alternative is to borrow the funds to purchase the asset, then the benefit of leasing depends on its after-tax cost compared with the after-tax cost of borrowing. Lease payments are tax deductible as a business expense, provided the asset is used to derive taxable income. However, don't be dazzled by the tax deductions if the after-tax cost of leasing is greater than the after-tax cost of borrowing. When a lease runs out, you don't own the asset. *Residual value* is an estimate of the value of the asset at the end of the lease period. You indemnify the lessor for the agreed residual value when they sell the asset. Most lessors, however, will accept an offer to buy the asset for its residual value at the end of the lease.

Leasing arrangements are usually more liberal than loans. While a bank generally requires a longer business history before granting a loan, many leasing companies evaluate your credit history over a shorter period. This can be a significant advantage for a start-up business. There are some things you should be looking for when you negotiate a lease. The term is typically between 24 and 48 months, depending on the asset. The shorter the term of a lease, or the lower the agreed residual value, the higher will be the monthly lease payments. Make sure you understand the full cost over the entire term of the lease, including any initial down payment, monthly lease payments, security deposit, insurance premiums, and service or repair costs?

There are other forms of leasing that may be relevant for your business. *Fleet leasing* is a possibility if your business has five or more passenger and light commercial vehicles. The services generally include vehicle sourcing, maintenance, management and disposal. One fixed monthly rental payment is made for the fleet. *Novated leasing* is designed to finance motor vehicles as part of salary packaging arrangements for your staff. They have the use of the vehicle plus the benefit of paying for it with pre-tax salary. Your commitment is to make the lease payments, which you deduct from the employee's salary package. If they leave your employment, they take the vehicle and the lease with them. An alternative to mortgage finance is the *sale and leaseback* of existing properties. The procedure is to sell a freehold property to a financial institution and then lease it back. You get the use of the property, you have the cash in hand, and the lease payments are tax deductible.

Equity capital

Equity capital is money invested in a business by its owners. You obtain equity capital in the first instance by putting your own money into the business. Later, you can increase the equity capital in the business by investing more of your own money or reinvesting some of the profits. You can also raise additional equity capital by selling part of your business.

Internal equity capital

The principal source of internal equity capital for a small business is the owner's money. For some individuals, it will be their life savings. For others, it will be money that has been borrowed on a personal basis in order to provide equity capital for the business. Another source of internal equity capital retained profits.

External equity capital

Very few small businesses ever seek external equity financing. However, if the need for equity capital exceeds the amounts available from the owner and the retained earnings of the business, then external equity capital may offer the only means by which the firm can expand its financial base. Some small business operators have relatives or acquaintances with spare cash who are willing to invest in the business. There are two sides to making business partners out of those with whom you have a personal relationship. They may be a great source of financial and emotional support, or they may meddle in the business by annoying you with incessant questions or unwanted advice.

Another source of external equity capital is private investors known as *business angels*. These are individuals who are prepared to provide equity capital in the form of share capital or partnership capital for a worthwhile venture. Not only do they provide equity capital, but they can also offer the benefit of their skills, experience, and network contacts. A business angel with experience in your line of business can be a big asset as well as a source of capital. Business angels tend to work informally by seeking investment opportunities through a network of personal contacts. For this reason, they are not always easy to locate. Ask your accountant, solicitor, and other financial advisers if they can help you locate an equity investor. There are websites that provide matching services for businesses and angel investors such as Business Angels at ***businessangels.com.au*** and the Angel Investment Network at ***australianinvestmentnetwork.com***.

Government grants

Commonwealth and state governments offer a number of grant programmes designed to help small businesses. In the right circumstances, government grants can be a great way to finance the growth of your business. However, there is a misconception that government grants are an easy source of 'free' money. On the contrary, applying for government funding can be a demanding and time-consuming process with no guarantee of success.

The first step is to find out what is available. The Commonwealth government website at ***business.gov.au/grants-and-programs*** lists all government-related grant programmes. Industry associations are also an excellent source of information about grants for their industry sector.

If you decide to apply for a government grant, there are a few things you can do to avoid disappointment. First, make sure you are eligible for the grant. Some grant programmes restrict what they will fund, so you don't want to go to all the effort of making an application only to be told you are not eligible. Second, give yourself plenty of time. It is not unusual to spend several weeks preparing an application. It is also not unusual for it to take several months to get an answer. Third, word your application carefully. The people who evaluate grant applications are looking for key words related to eligibility and the way in which you propose to use the grant. Clues about key words can generally be found in the description of the grant programme. Fourth, most grants require you to contribute up to 50 per cent of the costs of a project. Make sure you have access to matching funds or have another funding source arranged to demonstrate that you can meet your part if a grant is approved. Last, grants come with an obligation to report key milestones and furnish proof about how you used the money. Ensure your record keeping system is up to scratch and keep copies of all receipts, invoices, and other documentation in case you are audited.

Taxation

If ever there was a disincentive to operating a small business, it is taxation. The problem is not just the amount of tax you have to pay, but the mountain of paperwork that it takes to comply with the requirements of the ATO. The ATO has publications and other information for small businesses available on its website at *ato.gov.au*. The taxation system affects practically every phase of business, and trying to keep up with the ever-changing legislation and legal precedents can be exasperating. In order to minimise your tax burden and ease the administrative nightmare, you should engage a taxation consultant who is familiar with businesses like yours. In most cases, this will be your accountant.

A TFN is issued by the ATO to identify each taxpayer. If you have decided to operate your business as a sole trader, then you will use your individual TFN for both your personal and business dealings with the ATO. If you have decided to operate your business as a partnership, company or trust, then you will need to apply for a separate TFN.

Business records are required by law for taxation purposes. They must be kept in the English language, and they must be retained for at least five years. Consult your accountant or tax agent about which records you need to keep. They can also give you advice about the most efficient and economical means for complying with the ATO's record keeping requirements.

Pay-as-you-go (PAYG)

PAYG is a single, integrated system for reporting and paying the Goods and Services Tax (GST), withholding obligations, income tax instalments, and FBT instalments. If you are registered for the GST, then you report most of your tax entitlements and obligations under the PAYG system on one form called a *Business Activity Statement* (BAS). If you are not registered for the GST, then you lodge an *Instalment Activity Statement*. The ATO sends you an activity statement personalised for your business with some parts already filled in including the tax period it covers and when you need to lodge it.

The BAS asks you to record the total amount of GST that is payable on the goods and services that you sold during the tax period. You also record the total amount of credits for the GST that you paid on the goods and services you bought for use in your business. The difference between your GST payable and your GST credits is the amount you owe or will be refunded.

Withholding obligations are amounts you withhold from payments to others and remit to the ATO as part of your activity statement. The two main withholding obligations are employee deductions and payments to other businesses for which no ABN is quoted on their invoice. If you employ staff, you are required to deduct income tax from their salary, wages, and other payments. The types and rates of withholding payments are set out in the withholding schedules (tax tables) published on the ATO website. If a business supplies goods or services to you and does not quote an ABN on their invoice, then you are also required to withhold tax from your payment to the supplier at the top marginal rate and remit it to the ATO as part of your Business Activity Statement.

PAYG instalments are payable for income tax, GST, and taxes withheld when you lodge your Business Activity Statement. The final amounts payable to the ATO are reconciled when you lodge your annual returns and claim a credit for your instalments. You generally have a choice at the beginning of each tax year between paying instalment amounts calculated by the ATO or calculating the instalment amounts yourself based on your actual figures.

Goods and services tax (GST)

The Goods and Services Tax (GST) is a broad-based tax of 10 per cent on the value of most goods and services sold in Australia. If your annual turnover is $75,000 or more, you are legally required to register for the GST and you will need an ABN to do this. You should consider the benefits of registering for the GST even if your turnover is less than $75,000. By registering for the GST, you are entitled to claim input tax credits for the amount of GST included in the things you buy to use in your business. If you are not registered, you cannot claim the input tax credits. You can register for the GST online at the ATO website or through your registered tax agent. The final consumer bears the cost of GST, not the business providing the goods and services. Be sure to charge GST each time you make a sale. If you don't add GST to your prices, you will be out of pocket when it comes time to remit your GST to the Tax Office. Similarly, it is essential to keep track of your purchases to claim GST credits.

Income tax

Income tax is imposed by the Commonwealth government and collected by the ATO. The *Income Tax Assessment Act* defines the method of assessment of taxable income and the deductions that are allowed. The *Income Tax Act* sets the rates of tax to be levied depending on the legal form of organisation in which you operate. Both Acts are amended each year in the Commonwealth budget. You are required to furnish an income tax return to the ATO each year.

Individual taxpayers are levied under the PAYG system, whereby tax instalments are deducted from salaries and wages as they are received from the employer. However, a taxpayers' final tax liability for the year is not determined until they submit their annual tax return to the ATO and receive an income tax assessment notice. The amount of tax assessed and the amount of tax instalments already paid are reconciled resulting in either an additional payment or a refund. A sole proprietor includes their business income in their individual tax return.

A partnership information return is filed with the ATO even though no tax is payable on it. Each partner then includes their share of the partnership's taxable income in their individual tax return. A trustee is also required to furnish the ATO with an information return for a trust. Its purpose is to disclose the income of the trust and its distribution among the beneficiaries.

A company pays company tax and is required to lodge a company tax return. Since a company is a separate legal entity, its tax liability is determined separately from the tax liability of its shareholders. The dividend imputation system enables companies to pass on profits to shareholders in the form of franked dividends. A franked dividend means that a shareholder receives a tax credit for tax paid by the company on the income from which the dividend was paid. This enables the owners of small companies to achieve the best after-tax balance between salaries, dividends, and retained earnings. This legislation imposes a number of obligations on companies, so get professional advice.

Australia's income tax system works on the basis of self-assessment. This means that the ATO accepts the accuracy of the information you provide and calculates your tax liability accordingly. However, the ATO may ask you to provide the records to substantiate your tax return later. Keep in mind that activity statements are different from income tax returns. Although you report your PAYG income tax instalments, you must also lodge an income tax return.

Capital gains tax

Gains on the sale of some assets are subject to capital gains tax. You make a capital gain or loss when you sell an asset such as your business premises or goodwill. Capital gains tax does not generally apply to depreciating assets such as tools or motor vehicles because these are included in your income tax. A gain or loss is essentially equal to the difference between the proceeds of the sale and the cost of the asset. There is rollover relief from capital gains tax for small business owners who sell assets in order to buy other assets for use in a business, or who wish to sell the business in order to retire.

Fringe benefits tax

FBT applies to benefits provided to an employee that are not included in the salaries and wages withholding system. The FBT is payable by the employer based on the value of the benefit. If you are subject to FBT, then you will need to register with the ATO and lodge an FBT return. The ATO publishes a guide on its website that explains what FBT is and how to calculate it, and provides detailed information about the different kinds of fringe benefits and how they are treated.

Superannuation guarantee

When you employ staff, you are required to pay a superannuation contribution for your eligible employees. This also applies to contractors if more than 50 per cent of their contract is for labour. This is called the *Superannuation Guarantee*. Superannuation obligations under an industrial award count toward the minimum level of contributions, but an employee's own contributions do not.

Information about the superannuation guarantee is on the ATO website at ***ato.gov.au/super***.

State taxes

There are taxes and levies imposed by state governments that may apply to your business. The main ones are stamp duty and payroll tax. Refer to your state government website to find information on the taxes in your state. Stamp duty is levied on certain transactions, such as leases of commercial premises, mortgages, insurance policies, and transfers of property such as businesses or real estate. It is levied according to the value of the transaction. It is important to consider the impact of stamp duty if you are buying or selling a business. Payroll tax is levied on employers by state governments based on the amount of payroll expenditure. All states have an exemption threshold, but it is different in each state. If your payroll exceeds the threshold, you need to register with your state's revenue office and submit a periodic payroll tax return.

Facing a tax audit

If there is anything that can strike terror in the hearts of most individuals it is the thought of a tax audit. To lessen the possibility of an adverse audit, it generally pays to have your tax returns prepared by your accountant. It is up to you, however, to review your tax returns to ensure they are correct. You also need to keep your tax records for at least five years. If you receive a letter from the ATO or your state tax authority asking you to present yourself and your records for an audit, the following tips will help you get through it with a minimum of anxiety.

- Don't ignore it – whatever you do, don't ignore the letter informing you of an upcoming audit. If they don't hear from you, they will assume you are in the wrong and things can quickly escalate.
- Be prepared – the desk audit is the most common form of review. You will be asked to bring records that document the information contained in your tax return. Review your records before the appointment and prepare yourself to answer questions.
- Stay calm – your meeting with the ATO or state government representative may feel a bit adversarial, but it will not help your case if you become hostile. Remember, they are only doing their job.
- Stick to the point – answer only the questions asked and don't offer any additional information. This is not the time for a casual chat because anything you say may open up new issues leading to further investigations.

Call in your accountant or tax adviser if you need help. If you are only asked to provide documentary substantiation and you have it, then you can probably handle the audit on your own. If it is something more complex, then you should ask your accountant or tax adviser to assist you by helping you prepare for the audit and accompanying you to the meeting.

Summary

Lenders want to make loans to businesses that are solvent, profitable, and liquid. Your balance sheet, income statement, and cash flow budget are the lender's tools for determining how well you meet these criteria. Short-term borrowing is generally used to finance current assets such as working capital. Long-term borrowing is generally used to finance non-current assets such as vehicles or property. Leasing is an alternative to borrowing, especially if you prefer regular monthly lease payments compared with a single lump sum purchase. Internal equity capital is money you invest in a business including reinvesting some of the profits. External equity comes from selling part of your business to another party such as a business angel. Government grants can also be a source of cash for some businesses, but applying for government funding can be a demanding process with no guarantee of success. The taxation system affects practically every phase of business, and keeping up with the ever-changing legislation should be part of your accountant's service. They can help you comply with the pay-as-you-go system, the goods and services tax, income tax, capital gains tax, FBT, and other obligations. They can also help if you are audited by the tax office.

Part D

Reality check

Do the financial projections make sense?

An idea is not commercially viable unless the numbers make sense. The purpose of these questions is to evaluate the financial projections for transforming an idea into a going concern. These questions may require a little homework, so get some help if you need it from someone with financial expertise. The questions are designed to find answers to five important questions.

- What revenue can I expect?
- What investment in assets is required, and how will they be financed?
- Will the business be profitable?
- What level of sales will it take to breakeven?
- When will the business be cash flow positive?

An idea starts to become exciting when the numbers reveal that the start-up capital required is realistic, profits are attractive, the breakeven point is low, and cash flow is positive. Answering these questions not only satisfies the need to forecast the financial outcomes, but it will also help you decide if the idea is worth pursuing any further.

Revenue

The revenue forecast builds on your previous responses for anticipated demand, market acceptance and market strength. If the revenue forecast is way off the mark, then it will flow through the entire financial performance evaluation. However, it is not realistic to expect it to be perfectly accurate either. Here is an example.

Step 1	What is the customer for this product?
	Let's say, **households**.
Step 2	How many households are in the target market area?
	Let's say, **10,000 households**.

DOI: 10.4324/9781003394808-21

Step 3   What is the average annual number of purchases per household for this type of product? Let's say, **12 units per year**.

Step 4   What is the average price that customers are willing to pay for this product? Let's say, **$50 per unit.**

Step 5   What is the annual market potential for this product in this market?

10,000 households x 12 units per year x $50 per unit = **$6,000,000.**

Step 6   What share of this market can I confidently expect to capture? Let's say, **50 per cent**.

Step 7   What is my estimate of potential annual sales revenue? $6,000,000 annual sales x 50 per cent = **$3,000,000.**

36. A sales revenue forecast for my idea . . .

    a)   is complete and integrated into a blueprint for the business.
    b)   is complete but not yet integrated into a blueprint for the business.
    c)   has been started but is not finished yet.
    d)   is unnecessary because it is all in my head.
    e)   I don't know what the sales revenue is likely to be.

Investment and financing

The revenue forecast establishes the expected level of activity in the business. We need to identify the assets that are going to be needed to support that level of activity and how they will be financed. We can do this by projecting a balance sheet that contains the assets required by the business, the money that will be borrowed by the business, and the owners' investment in the business.

- The investment in current assets consists of the working capital required to maintain a smooth operating cycle.
- The investment in fixed assets consists of the plant and equipment that are required to undertake the level of activity in the revenue forecast.
- The difference between the investment in assets and the owners' equity is how much debt financing, if any, will be needed.

37. Will the financial structure for my idea consist mainly of . . .

    a)   current assets financed with owner's equity?
    b)   fixed assets financed with owner's equity?
    c)   fixed assets financed with borrowing?
    d)   current assets financed with borrowing?
    e)   I don't know what the financial structure will be.

Profitability

A projected income statement is used to forecast profitability. It uses the revenue forecast together with the expenses incurred in obtaining the revenue and shows the resulting profit or loss.

- The sales revenue forecast is the starting point for a projected income statement.
- The cost of the goods or services that are sold is subtracted from the revenue forecast to arrive at gross profit.
- Next come the operating expenses of running the business at the level of activity in the sales revenue forecast.
- When operating expenses have been subtracted from gross profit, the difference is net profit before tax.
- After income tax has been calculated, the last entry is net profit after tax.

38. Will commercialising my idea be likely to . . .

    a) earn an exceptionally good profit?
    b) earn a fair profit?
    c) incur a loss in the first year?
    d) incur a loss in the first two or three years?
    e) I don't know how profitable my idea is likely to be.

Breakeven

The dynamics of breakeven is a powerful tool for forecasting profitability. When the sales revenue forecast exceeds the breakeven point, the prospects for a successful business are enhanced.

- Rearrange the projected income statement into fixed and variable costs.
- Calculate the contribution margin
- Find the breakeven point by dividing the fixed costs by the contribution margin.

39. Is the sales revenue forecast for my idea . . .

    a) well above the breakeven point?
    b) moderately above the breakeven point?
    c) about the same as the breakeven point?
    d) below the breakeven point?
    e) I don't know what the breakeven point is likely to be.

Cash flow

If forecasted cash flow is positive, then commercialising an idea begins to look feasible. But if forecasted cash flow is negative, then there is a risk that the idea may end in failure. In this last question, you need to do a cash flow budget for your idea and interpret the results.

40. Will operating cash flow for my idea be positive . . .

    a)   from the first day?
    b)   within a couple of months?
    c)   by the end of the first year?
    d)   sometime after the first year?
    e)   I don't know when cash flow will become positive.

Feedback

The purpose of these questions is to help you reach a judgement about the financial viability of commercialising an idea. This plays a crucial role in deciding if you want to take an idea any further. The key is to reflect on each of the questions and how you have responded to them.

It is vital to have a revenue forecast for physical activity, such as units sold or services rendered, as well as for dollar sales. Responses 'a' and 'b' satisfy this requirement, but the others do not. Without a revenue forecast, it is not possible to answer the remaining questions.

For investment and financing, responses 'a' and 'b' represent a financial structure with the lowest risk because there is no borrowing. Responses 'c' and 'd' are possible, but they are also riskier because money must be borrowed. Response 'e' means there is work yet to be completed on the financial projections.

For profitability, responses 'a' and 'b' are encouraging because they represent immediate profitability. Responses 'c' and 'd' are more of a concern because commercialising the idea must ride out some period of losses. Response 'e' means there is work yet to be completed on the financial projections.

For breakeven, responses 'a' and 'b' are encouraging because there is a margin of safety between the revenue forecast and the breakeven point. Response 'c' is problematic because it means neither profit nor loss. Response 'd' is a concern because commercialising the idea will result in some losses. Response 'e' means there is work yet to be completed on the financial projections.

For cash flow, responses 'a' and 'b' are encouraging because the idea is forecast to be cash flow positive relatively quickly. Responses 'c' and 'd' are more of a concern because cash reserves need to be available to keep operating until cash flow becomes positive. Response 'e' means there is work yet to be completed on the financial projections.

Is there anything that can be done to strengthen the financial strategy by finding ways to improve some of the responses? Unless you are satisfied that the blueprint for commercialising an idea will become cash positive and profitable, then abandonment may be the only logical conclusion. These questions will also become part of the Commercial Feasibility Rating in the Appendix.

Appendix
Commercial feasibility rating

The purpose of the commercial feasibility rating is to help you exercise your judgement about whether you want to move on to the next stage of developing an idea into a business. The value you get from it depends on how objectively you apply it. It is easy to get excited by the prospects of a new idea, so you need to be aware of the danger that your judgement might be distorted by your enthusiasm.

The commercial feasibility rating provides you with an overall measure of the commercial potential of an idea. It should not be taken too literally, however, because it is an initial evaluation based on your responses to the questions in this book. Refer back to your responses to the questions in each of the reality check sections. Record your responses on the answer sheet on the next page. You may wish to revise your responses to some of the questions before making a final selection.

The commercial feasibility rating should not be regarded as a one-off exercise. An idea with commercial potential is a valuable asset. The commercial feasibility rating is a tool that can be repeated as often as necessary to help you refine an idea until you decide whether or not to take it further.

Answer sheet

External risks						Market strength					
1. Compliance risk	a	b	c	d	e	21. Differentiation	a	b	c	d	e
2. Technology risk	a	b	c	d	e	22. Value	a	b	c	d	e
3. Economic risk	a	b	c	d	e	23. Customers	a	b	c	d	e
4. Political risk	a	b	c	d	e	24. Suppliers	a	b	c	d	e
5. Dependence risk	a	b	c	d	e	25. Competitors	a	b	c	d	e

Internal risks						Expertise					
6. Planning risk	a	b	c	d	e	26. Marketing expertise	a	b	c	d	e
7. Marketing risk	a	b	c	d	e	27. Technical expertise	a	b	c	d	e
8. Deliverables risk	a	b	c	d	e	28. Financial expertise	a	b	c	d	e
9. Liquidity risk	a	b	c	d	e	29. Functional expertise	a	b	c	d	e
10. Personal risk	a	b	c	d	e	30. Managerial expertise	a	b	c	d	e

Anticipated demand						Resources					
11. Market size	a	b	c	d	e	31. Financial resources	a	b	c	d	e
12. Market growth	a	b	c	d	e	32. Physical resources	a	b	c	d	e
13. Market stability	a	b	c	d	e	33. Human resources	a	b	c	d	e
14. Commercial lifespan	a	b	c	d	e	34. Critical information	a	b	c	d	e
15. Spinoffs	a	b	c	d	e	35. Help and assistance	a	b	c	d	e

Market acceptance						Financial performance					
16. Need	a	b	c	d	e	36. Revenue	a	b	c	d	e
17. Recognition	a	b	c	d	e	37. Investment	a	b	c	d	e
18. Compatibility	a	b	c	d	e	38. Profitability	a	b	c	d	e
19. Complexity	a	b	c	d	e	39. Breakeven	a	b	c	d	e
20. Distribution	a	b	c	d	e	40. Cash flow	a	b	c	d	e

To calculate the commercial feasibility rating, count the number of a, b, c, d, and e responses and convert them to numerical scores according to the following scale: a = 5, b = 4, c = 3, d = 2, and e = 1. Sum the total of your scores and divide it by 2.

$$
\begin{aligned}
&\underline{\hspace{2cm}} \text{ a's} \times 5 = \underline{\hspace{2cm}} \\
&\underline{\hspace{2cm}} \text{ b's} \times 4 = \underline{\hspace{2cm}} \\
&\underline{\hspace{2cm}} \text{ c's} \times 3 = \underline{\hspace{2cm}} \\
&\underline{\hspace{2cm}} \text{ d's} \times 2 = \underline{\hspace{2cm}} \\
&\underline{\hspace{2cm}} \text{ e's} \times 1 = \underline{\hspace{2cm}}
\end{aligned}
$$

Total	_____
Divided by	2
Commercial Feasibility Rating	_____

The commercial feasibility rating is an overall evaluation of commercial potential. The objective is to help you come to a conclusion about the commercial potential of an idea and whether you think it is a business opportunity worth pursuing. It will fall into one of three categories, which are interpreted in terms of a traffic light.

Green light

If your idea scored 80 or more, then its commercial potential appears good, and further investment of time, energy, and money is likely to be rewarded. A commercial feasibility rating in the lower half of this range (80–89) generally represents a moderate level of risk, a viable market, a sound operating strategy, and realistic financial projections, but it could still have some important concerns that need to be resolved. A commercial feasibility rating in the upper half of this range (90 and above) generally represents an acceptable level of risk, excellent market viability, a robust operating strategy, and solid financial projections.

This does not mean that an idea with a commercial feasibility rating of 80 or more is automatically ready to go. It means the idea has passed this reality test, and it is likely that you have found a business opportunity that is worth pursuing. The next stage is researching and compiling a blueprint for putting the idea into operation.

Yellow light

If your idea scored between 60 and 79, then its commercial potential appears marginal. However, it may nevertheless warrant some degree of cautious consideration. A commercial feasibility rating in this range means further development should be limited to resolving the sources of poor responses. A commercial feasibility rating in the upper half of this range (70–79) generally represents satisfactory market viability, but there are typically some concerns about risk and/or problems with the operating strategy and the financial projections. A commercial feasibility rating in this range is likely to have enough potential to warrant further limited and cautious development. A commercial feasibility rating in the lower half of this range (60–69) generally represents marginal market viability, significant risks, and/or difficulty with the operating strategy and the financial projections. It is unlikely that it will have enough potential to warrant further development unless major steps can be taken to improve its commercial feasibility rating.

Red light

If an idea scored under 60, then its commercial potential appears to be poor and further consideration is generally not recommended. A commercial feasibility rating below 60 generally represents unacceptable risks, an inadequate market, or an impractical operating strategy leading to unsatisfactory financial projections. In this situation, abandonment may be the best course of action. Sometimes it is the opportunity itself that is flawed, and sometimes the flaw is in the marketplace. Either way, it is better to reach this conclusion now rather than after you have wasted your time, money, and effort for no return. Alternatively, a poor commercial feasibility rating at this stage could be an indication that there has not been enough research to give the idea an objective evaluation.

Index

manufacturing 121–125
market: acceptance 76–80; capture 11; ideas 10; niche 50; position 50–51; strength 80–84
marketing: methods 57–72; mix 55–56; strategy 49–56
mentor 32–33
mobile devices 109
mobile marketing 71

name 22–24
newsletter 57–58

occupational health and safety 29
online directory 68–69, 107
online operations 100–110
operating constraints 11, 127–134
operating strategy 89–125
outsourcing 123–124

pandemic 7–9
partnership 19–20
Pay-As-You-Go (PAYG) 156–157
personal selling 62–63
Pinterest 67
planning *see* blueprint
point of sale system (POS) 119
premises 24–26
pricing 53–54, 93–94
product ideas 9
production 123
product strategy 51–52
profitability 146–148
promotion 52–53, 91–92, 106–109
publicity 58

radical ideas 10
resources 131–133
retail 111–120
risk 10, 37–45

safety 7–8
search engine 106–107
serviced office 25
services 9, 89–99
small business agency 34
social media 66–68
sole proprietorship 19
solicitor 30
sponsorship 58–59
start-up 19–29
stock control 118–119, 124

target market 73–85
taxation 155–160
Tax File Number (TFN) 24
trade association 33–34
trademark 24
TripAdvisor 69
trust 21–22
Twitter 67–68

virtual marketplace 68–69, 100–101

website 69–70, 101–107
workers' compensation insurance 29

Yelp 69
YouTube 68

Printed in the United States
by Baker & Taylor Publisher Services